More Than 100 Ways to

LEARNER-CENTERED

LITERACY

Second Edition

More Than 100 Ways to
LEARNER-CENTERED
LITERACY

Second Edition

Laura Lipton
Deborah Hubble

CORWIN
PRESS
A SAGE Company

For information:

Corwin Press
A SAGE Company
2455 Teller Road
Thousand Oaks,
   California 91320
www.corwinpress.com

SAGE Ltd.
1 Oliver's Yard
55 City Road
London, EC1Y 1SP
United Kingdom

SAGE India Pvt. Ltd.
B 1/I 1 Mohan Cooperative
   Industrial Area
Mathura Road,
   New Delhi 110 044
India

SAGE Asia-Pacific Pte. Ltd.
33 Pekin Street #02-01
Far East Square
Singapore 048763

Library of Congress Cataloging-in-Publication Data

Lipton, Laura.
  More than 100 ways to learner-centered literacy / Laura Lipton and Deborah Hubble. — 2nd ed.
      p. cm.
  Rev. ed. of: More than 50 ways to learner-centered literacy. c1997.
  Includes bibliographical references and index.
  ISBN 978-1-4129-5784-7 (cloth) — ISBN 978-1-4129-5783-0 (pbk.)
  1. Language arts (Preschool)—United States. 2. Language arts (Elementary)—United States. 3. Active learning—United States. 4. Literacy—United States. I. Hubble, Deborah. II. Lipton, Laura. More than 50 ways to learner-centered literacy. III. Title.

  LB1140.5.L3L56 2009
  372.6—dc22

2008017821

08 09 10 11 10 9 8 7 6 5 4 3 2 1

Acquisitions Editor:	Cathy Hernandez
Editorial Assistant:	Ena Rosen and Megan Bedell
Production Editor:	Appingo Publishing Services
Cover Designer:	Scott Van Atta

Contents

Acknowledgments

Corwin Press gratefully acknowledges the contributions of the following reviewers:

Jane Ching Fung, First-Grade Teacher
Alexander Science Center School
Los Angeles, CA

Leigh Hall, Assistant Professor, Literacy Education
University of North Carolina, Chapel Hill
Chapel Hill, NC

Vicki Seeger, Literacy Coach
Seaman Unified School District 345
Topeka, KS

Gayle Simoneaux, Teacher
Mimosa Park Elementary School
Luling, LA

Debbie Smith, Teacher
Lady's Island Elementary School
Beaufort, SC

About the Authors

Laura Lipton, EdD, is codirector of MiraVia, LLC, a publishing and development firm in Sherman, Connecticut. Laura is an international consultant whose writing, research, and seminars focus on effective and innovative instructional practices and on building professional and organizational capacities for enhanced learning. Laura engages with schools and school districts, designing and conducting workshops on organizational development, learning-focused instruction, literacy development, and strategies to support beginning teachers. She applies her extensive experience with adult learners to workshops and seminars conducted throughout the United States, Canada, Europe, Australia, and New Zealand on such topics as learning-focused relationships, data-driven dialogue, teacher leadership, action research, and learning-focused mentoring.

Laura is author and coauthor of numerous publications related to organizational and professional development, learning-focused schools, and literacy development.

Deborah Hubble is currently an assistant principal in the Katy Independent School District (Houston). She also serves as a writer of monthly research abstracts for Effective Schools, a nationally acclaimed school reform organization. Her school-related passions include creating authentic literacy experiences for children, providing professional development in reading and writing workshop approaches, and supporting and educating stakeholders through organizational change and school reform. With experiences of being a special education teacher, district language arts coordinator, elementary school librarian, elementary school literacy coach, and mom to four young children, Deb's interest in learner-centered literacy has been pursued for twenty years.

Introduction

All learners, whether they are teachers or students, must be willing to live their learning in public so that it is a source of demonstration for others.
—Kathy Short and Carolyn Burke

REASONS WE READ

We read to explore the world, to make connections between descriptive information and our own experience. We read to be informed because we are curious about so many things, and text resources both stimulate and satisfy that drive. We read because it is empowering; we ask our own questions and seek our own answers. And we read to share the adventures of others; as we become more knowledgeable about the world—present and past—we come to understand ourselves in relation to it. Reading confirms and expands who we are and who we might become. Reading validates our views and alters them.

This book is based on this philosophical and practical sense of purpose for becoming a reader. It is not about sounding out words, memorization, regurgitation, or skimming the surface of a story. Rather it treats reading as a process that produces connection, discovery, and deep understanding. To be literate is to be thoughtful and to engage thoughtfully as a reader, writer, listener, and speaker. This book offers methods, ideas, and strategies intended to create literate human beings, not just skillful readers.

Inside, you will find ideas generated from discussions with teachers from the United States and Canada, visits to their classrooms, and observations of their interactions with students. This book is designed for educators making their maiden voyage into the land of learner-centered instruction; those who are actively engaged in exploring; and those long-time residents who are continually seeking to expand their horizons. The book is meant to encourage, support, stimulate, facilitate, provoke, and provide.

The book is divided into six sections, each containing ideas for the following:

1. Designing a literate environment
2. Orchestrating student interaction
3. Developing strategies for fluency
4. Nurturing lifelong learners
5. Assessing student growth
6. Leading learning-focused conversations

In each section, there are strategies that take little preparation and provide a risk-free way of initiating beginning experiences with learner-centered instruction, strategies that take a little more effort and require additional planning, and strategies that require extensive preparation and a readjustment or reprioritization of instructional time.

Although the sections are organized from the least to the most complex strategies, there is no intended better or worse, right or wrong, or embedded goal to reorchestrate the classroom. All of the strategies described in this volume are for teachers who want to provide rich literacy learning for their students and whose classrooms and instructional methods reflect the principles of learner-centered instruction at any level.

New in this second edition is a special supplement for literacy specialists, with practical tips and specific strategies for collaboratively building and sharing expertise in practice. Based on Lipton and Wellman's learning-focused continuum (2003), this section focuses on patterns and practices for adult-to-adult interactions.

LEARNER-CENTERED INSTRUCTION: A PHILOSOPHY, NOT AN INSTRUCTIONAL MODEL

A learner-centered *approach* to instruction is an attitude, not a method. It is about the joy of learning together and self-confidently pursuing new discoveries. Learner-centered *instruction* is built on learners' questions, reflections, and experimentations as they engage in meaningful and relevant activities. The learner-centered *curriculum* exists as an outgrowth of those experiences.

In a natural environment, language is used for self-expression, to share and process experiences, and to make sense of the world. Students should be exposed to the purposes of language in school as well. To support students' developing control over the conventions of language, an environment that encourages and supports risk taking and experimentation must be established. Opportunities for practicing and integrating new learning are structured, successful attempts are applauded, and temporary failures are constructively examined and integrated.

Learner-centered instruction is the expression of the way in which teachers create learning opportunities for their students and themselves. The ideas in this book are designed to support those endeavors.

SEVEN PRINCIPLES OF LITERACY DEVELOPMENT

The activities and strategies explored in this book are based on seven key principles of literacy development. These principles have been extrapolated from current research and practice in reading instruction and cognitive science.

1. Making Meaning Is Always the Goal of Communication

Simply put, learners construct meaning while reading and listening, and express meaning while speaking and writing.

Making meaning is always the goal. Although this principle seems straightforward, teachers often send conflicting messages to children about reading, writing, listening, and speaking. If making meaning is always the goal, teaching contextual and semantic cues becomes more important than sounding out a word. Accepting temporary or invented spelling allows freedom of expression without constraining young writers to using only the words they can spell correctly.

2. Children Learn Language Conventions by Learning Language

We don't learn language by watching it; we learn it by actively using it. The reading process is best learned by using complete forms of written language, not by learning isolated skills. Activities should be structured in purposeful, authentic tasks, and ample opportunities for children to listen, speak, read, and write should be provided. As students engage in these processes, they develop the capacity to solve new problems by using increasingly familiar strategies and cues. They begin to notice new things about words and the conventions of language and to link these discoveries to previously learned information and procedures. These discoveries become reference points for future learning.

3. A Learner's Experience Is a Key Factor in the Construction of Meaning

Reading is an interaction between the print on a page and the knowledge of the reader. Readers construct meaning during reading by using their prior knowledge and experience. Imagine this newspaper headline: "Vikings Slaughter Dolphins." Most people in the United States would automatically think of a football game. However, for someone who knows nothing about football, the headline might elicit a description of a historical event.

The foundations of children's literacy are in their home environments. Capitalizing on the language experiences children bring to school is critical to their success as learners.

4. Choice Encourages Commitment to Learning

When students are allowed to choose their learning options, they develop a greater sense of commitment to their own learning, ownership of their work, and a higher level of responsibility. Knowledge of an individual student's needs and interests as well as sound professional judgment guide teachers in providing each student with some choice in reading and writing activities.

5. Error Reduction, Not Error Elimination, Is the Aim of Instruction

Learners gain as much from making mistakes as they do from being correct—maybe more! Therefore, it is important to offer an environment in which language is cultivated through experience and experimentation with specific feedback and sound learning strategies.

6. The Language Arts Are Integrated With Each Other and the Content Areas

Language is never context free. Effective literacy instruction keeps language whole and connected to a purpose. Literacy includes thinking, reading, writing, speaking, and listening. These cannot be separated into isolated skills in which students are drilled for mastery. Providing contextual experiences that connect children's lives to the world around them is vital. Further, functional communication on relevant topics includes information and interest in content areas. Content area instruction is a fertile place for students' developing literacy.

7. Assessment Is Learner Referenced, Providing Direction for Future Learning

Assessment in the learner-centered classroom is formative, developmental, and descriptive. Data about both the product and process of each student is gathered by the teacher through observation and short-cycle assessments. These data are interpreted to ascertain each child's growing repertoire of skills and strategies. There is a growth orientation, rather than a remedial one, and teachers look at what a child can do, as well as determine what she or he cannot do yet.

CREATING THE ENVIRONMENT: CONDITIONS FOR LANGUAGE LEARNING

A fundamental premise of learner-centered instruction is that language learning is a natural process. It is rare to encounter the parents of a six-month-old baby, for example, who express concern that their child may never learn to speak. They recognize that oral language is a process that develops over time. They intuitively know that, given daily oral interaction, this child will learn to speak—without ever having a worksheet! They respond with delight to all attempts at speech that the child makes; parents never say, "It's not *baba*; it's *blanket*." Instead, they praise the child and provide the appropriate modeling: "You want your blanket? What a clever girl you are to ask for it!" With continuous modeling and feedback, the child's oral language will become more and more sophisticated. Literacy learning follows a similar natural process. Yet, traditional reading programs have dissected the process into a sequence of isolated skills to be mastered before children are expected to be fluent readers and writers.

Learner-centered teachers strive to provide conditions for learning that echo those in which children learn to speak. To create the appropriate environment, the teacher organizes and structures experiences, demonstrates and models the conventions of language, and clarifies complex processes and information. The teacher is a reflective learner and colearner, a conference partner, a supportive coach.

Based on the work of Cambourne (1988) and others, we offer three key characteristics that should be consciously orchestrated by teachers committed to developing language learning, providing optimal literacy experiences, and ensuring student success. This book is designed to provide a plethora of ideas for creating these qualities in the learner-centered classroom.

High Expectations for All Learners

Learners are influenced, either enabled or limited, by the expectations of those around them, particularly respected adults and their peers. It is critical to convey to students the expectation that they will succeed at their learning tasks. Subtle messages that reading is difficult or complex can be daunting to young learners. Be conscious about conveying positive and high expectations to students.

Toward that end, error reduction, not error avoidance, is the goal of instruction. In fact, students learn a great deal from reflecting on their mistakes and developing strategies for not repeating them. Approximation, or process of trial and error as students strive for excellence, allows students to take risks and work confidently in struggling to meet learning challenges. Skillful teachers help students to learn from their errors, as well as their successes.

Developing self-reliant, self-regulating students is a key goal. Learners grow in these areas when they make their own choices and decisions about the when, how, and what of their learning tasks. Choices might include what to read or where, when, or how much; which new vocabulary words to focus on; whom to choose as a learning partner; and so on.

Learning-focused teachers build as much choice as possible into their instructional program.

Real-Life Reading in a Print-Rich Environment

Students need to be surrounded by a wide range of print and print materials. These materials might include labels, lists, charts, books, dictated stories, songs, and displays. Students should have access to print resources and a variety of reading materials, including trade books, magazines, newspapers, and advertising flyers. It is particularly beneficial when the classroom is filled with print that is based on students' shared experiences and relevant to students' needs and interests.

Clear, Purposeful Models With Rich Practice Opportunities and Relevant Feedback

Demonstrations are models of the conventional mechanics and usage of language. Teachers provide demonstrations whenever they write on the board, read aloud, or post messages. Demonstrations provide contextual models that enable learners to experience the conventions of language and language use in print and speech. Be explicit and think aloud so students can observe process as well as product.

Rich, diverse, and motivating activities offer students an opportunity to practice their developing control over their language learning. Rather than skill and drill, organize authentic, purposeful tasks in which students must exercise their expanding knowledge, skills, and attitudes.

Learners are encouraged and supported by specific, meaningful feedback that constructively guides them toward improvement. The aim is for learners to recognize areas for change, establish learning goals, and internalize the criteria for excellence.

Use rubrics developed with students to clarify expectations and give students clear standards. In this way, they learn to do their own gap analysis and set their own learning goals.

OVERVIEW OF THE BOOK

More Than 100 Ways to Learner-Centered Literacy is full of practical instructional ideas that can be modified for K–6 use. Although many of the ideas lend themselves especially well to a language arts curriculum, the activities and strategies are highly adaptable for use across content areas. After all, in every subject, the focus should be on the learners. Successful implementation of the ideas in this book is context dependent. We have included tips throughout the text to spark individual teachers' creativity.

Each section of the book provides strategies designed to fulfill one of five critical components of learner-centered education. Section 1, "Designing a Literate Environment," addresses design, structure, and climate. A literate environment is full of language and activity relevant and meaningful to the students—often in sharp contrast to the sterile surroundings of a traditional classroom.

Section 2, "Orchestrating Student Interaction," provides multiple examples of activities intended to promote collaborative work among students. Resting on current research supporting the social nature of learning, these activities enable learners of all ages to maximize one another's strengths and gain experience in working cooperatively—as the real world demands.

Section 3, "Developing Comprehension Fluency," incorporates the recommendations of the National Reading Panel (2000) for both explicit and blended strategy instruction. It includes classroom ideas that promote various thinking skills. Creative and critical thinking can be bolstered in any classroom when students are encouraged to continually make and confirm predictions, are involved in extended reading experiences, and are immersed in integrated thematic instruction.

Section 4 is titled "Nurturing Lifelong Learners." Even though from a global perspective the United States has a relatively high literacy rate, there is an alarmingly high rate of aliterate people: those persons who can read and write but never choose to do so. Learner-centered education uncovers the joy of learning, so education becomes a lifelong, personal quest—initiated by the learner! Activities in Section 4 have been successful in launching this love for literacy and learning. The teacher nurtures this lifelong love rather than coaxes students to complete their schoolwork.

Section 5, "Strategies for Assessing Student Growth," focuses on strategies for teachers rather than on activities for the classroom. It offers educators valid alternatives to traditional, standardized assessment. As teachers implement the activities described in Sections 1–4, it quickly becomes apparent that "fill-in-the-bubbles" tests can no longer adequately measure what students know and what they are capable of doing. Learner-centered teachers view assessment and instruction as a virtual cycle: One cannot occur without the other. This final instructional section discusses multiple strategies for implementing assessment techniques that naturally inform future instruction. Individual student achievement is of the highest importance, and this chapter is full of ideas for such measurement.

As a whole, these five sections provide a base for creating a learner-centered classroom. It is our hope that educators will read the text with their own students in mind and adapt the activities and strategies accordingly. We believe that in doing so, educators will transform the school experience for the learners of today and tomorrow.

New in this second edition, Section 6, "Leading Learning-Focused Conversations," provides tips and tools for leading the professional one-to-one and small-group work that focuses on the continual improvement of literacy teaching and learning. Strategies and practical suggestions are offered for working with both novice and experienced colleagues.

SECTION 1

Designing a Literate Environment

The classroom environment you create has a profound effect on the social, emotional, physical, and intellectual development of the children you teach. To gain a positive attitude towards school and learning, children must have visual stimulation, organization, space, and a feeling of warmth and security.

—Mindy Pollishuke

The learner-centered classroom is alive with activity. In it, students' learning capacity is nurtured and developed as they safely risk exploring and discovering. Teachers and students in the learner-centered classroom are colearners, immersed in the explorations of language and literature.

Visiting a learner-centered classroom may be daunting at first. Imagine a place where everyone is busily pursuing different activities—some in pairs, some individually, some in small groups. This scene may initially appear chaotic, but everyone in this learner-centered classroom is engaged in authentic tasks, purposefully pursuing ideas, information, and learning goals. Some students may be involved in listening activities, perhaps at listening stations with tape recorders or CDs; some students may be at the "publishing center" developing their written work using computers; some may be working with the teacher, one on one or in a small group; some may be developing a project, possibly a play or a poster; and some students may be working individually, reading, writing, or reflecting. The theme of the students' work is usually seen in their artwork, classroom displays, and writing, which surrounds the classroom.

The most important part of creating a literate environment is establishing a well-organized, stimulating, comfortable, and inviting classroom. A classroom library is the focal point of this print-rich environment. Most of the print in the classroom should be at the children's eye level. Specific teaching areas, preferably on a rug where all can gather, should be well defined and apparent for both small and large groups. The environment is designed to allow children to move about freely, indicating their internalization of routines and expectations.

Learning Language
by Using It

Children learn to read and write effectively only if they are admitted into a community of written language users, which I shall call the "literacy club," starting before the children are able to read or write a single word for themselves.

—Frank Smith

BACKGROUND

Immersing students in print by covering the classroom with words in all forms is a powerful way to use the environmental surround to support literacy learning. Years ago, we visited a bilingual classroom that offers a perfect example of this approach. In this effective classroom, when the students finished a book, they wrote the title and author on a construction paper cactus flower and stapled it to their own cactus streamer. Twenty six brightly colored streamers covered with flowers were suspended from the classroom ceiling as a reminder of all the books the class read.

The classroom walls were filled with students' writing. Large discovery charts across one wall displayed students' new knowledge about the Arctic. Each sentence frame read, "I was surprised to discover that _____." Each chart held about thirty interesting pieces of information about the Arctic gleaned from the children's reading and class discussions.

The math corner was filled with manipulatives and other materials, all labeled in Spanish. The directions for activities and behavior guides at that center were printed in Spanish as well. A large percentage of the math lessons were taught completely in Spanish by a bilingual partner teacher—and the English-speaking teacher is learning a second language along with her students.

Two important conditions for literacy learning in the learner-centered classroom are immersion in print and modeling the conventions of language use. In this classroom, students see their teacher as a learning model, struggling every day with the challenge of learning something new. Students have the opportunity to develop language literacy by being immersed in print, both in English and in Spanish.

Just as parents expect their toddlers to begin speaking as a result of being spoken to for ten to twelve months, learner-centered teachers expect young children to exhibit various literacy behaviors as a result of being read to and immersed in language. Early-childhood teachers make productive use of the emerging literacy abilities that children bring to school. Teachers of older children, also, value and build upon the reading, writing, and speaking abilities exhibited by the students.

1   Labels, Labels Everywhere

Print carries meaning; the same configuration of lines and squiggles conveys the same information each time it appears. Once students understand this concept, they have the key to becoming readers. One way to help promote this understanding is by using labels. Labels help learners connect print with objects and reinforce the concept that things have names that can be written down.

Label everything in your classroom: the closet, the window, the bookshelf, Mrs. Smith's desk, the door, the clock, and other objects.

Create role cards to label students' functions in cooperative groups, such as recorder, timekeeper, and encourager.

Brainstorm adjectives and descriptive phrases with the class and add them to the labels: the *storage* closet, the *dirty* window, the *expanding* bookshelf, the clock *that runs too slow*, and so on.

Students can also label events or behaviors with characteristics, which introduces humor, diffuses tension, and reinforces classroom behavioral norms. For example, if two students have a disagreement, the other students might give them the "stubborn" label! Or, on one of those days when you have left something out or neglected to do something, your students might label you "forgetful"!

After gaining experience with the labels in the classroom, children will often use the labels as *anchors* when attempting to write new words on their own. For example, they realize that the sound they want to write on their paper is the first sound they hear in the label that says "desk."

MATERIALS YOU WILL NEED

- 3" × 5" index cards
- Felt-tip markers
- Masking tape

2   Where in the Room Is It?

Visual discrimination is the capacity to see differences between letters, configurations of letter groups, and different words. Because reading involves various visual patterns (clusters of words, syllables, blends, letters), children need to develop the ability to visually discriminate to become more fluent readers. Children tend to operate on visual patterns in very diverse and personal ways, and beginning readers need approximately 100 exposures to a word before it becomes a *sight word*.

This game calls children's attention to the words around them and develops their visual discrimination. When making labels for various objects in the room (see Strategy 1: Labels, Labels Everywhere), make a smaller set of cards with the same words. Let students pick a card and search the room to find the corresponding label. By matching their card to the appropriate label in the classroom, children are sharpening their visual discrimination skills. While comparing their personal card next to a label in the classroom, they are visually processing to either confirm or reject the combination of letters on each card. This is similar to the reading experience in meaningful text: The reader samples the text visually and confirms or rejects his or her predictions about the words.

VARIATIONS

Create bingo cards and have students locate labels and cross out the corresponding words on their cards. Students can also work in small groups using a scavenger hunt format for Where in the Room Is It?

MATERIALS YOU WILL NEED

- 3" × 5" index cards cut in half
- Felt-tip markers

3   Wordstrings

A classroom rich in language has print displayed everywhere. Some of the print is teacher written and some is written by children. Word walls, language-experience charts, enlarged copies of poems from shared reading—all immerse children in language.

A clothesline is a simple and inexpensive way to capitalize on unused space in the classroom. Capture students' language on sheets of chart or butcher paper and string across the room or around its perimeter on a clothesline. These developing word lists provide stimulating, descriptive language created by the students' experiences. Students will return again and again to these familiar records of their developing knowledge, often imitating the teacher and using a pointer as they read the text.

To create a wordstring, paste an illustration or photograph on the center of a large piece of chart or butcher paper and hang it on a chalkboard or easel. Have students list all the words or short phrases that the picture brings to their minds on their own piece of paper. You may want to choose a picture that elicits emotional or aesthetic reactions. The complexity of the picture and the students' associations will vary based on their experience level.

Ask students to volunteer to share their words with the class. Write students' words on the chart paper, surrounding the picture, and hang it on the wordstring. Students can use the picture as a story starter. The displayed vocabulary will enhance their writing. Younger students can use the words to complete sentence frames that can be displayed on other wordstrings.

TECHNOLOGY OPTION

This activity can be modified by technology, as well. Gather students around the computer and use KidPix or Kidspiration software to develop the icons and supporting vocabulary words. After whole group demonstrations, students could create their own individual wordstrings during computer workstation time.

MATERIALS YOU WILL NEED

- Glue
- Photograph or illustration
- Chart or butcher paper
- Writing materials
- Felt-tip markers
- Clothesline
- Clothespins

4   String 'Em Up

Children need to see and hear language patterns repeatedly until the patterns become familiar and predictable. Pattern books, predictable stories, and songs are an effective source of consistent language patterns. Teachers promote the conventions of print (word separation, difference between letters and words, where a reader begins on a line, how to go from left to right, etc.) by using printed versions of patterns that children recognize auditorily. By connecting the patterns they have memorized with the printed word presented by the teacher, emergent readers begin to embark upon the road to reading independence.

A clothesline offers space to string up a story for chanting or shared reading, retelling, or discussion about sequence. Be sure to have plenty of colorful clothespins on hand!

Start with a favorite story. A class-created story works especially well. Reproduce the text from each page onto large chart paper. Be sure to duplicate the original spacing and print layout exactly.

Reread the story with the class.

Give each student, or pairs of students, one page to illustrate. They can use tempera paint or crayons. Talk with the children to be sure their planned illustration represents the meaning in the text.

As a class, organize the entire "book" across the clothesline and discuss sequence. Reread it frequently. Use the story to point out special words, phonetics, or punctuation conventions, such as quotation marks or exclamation points. You will notice the children reading it independently as well.

After a week or so, bind the story together and add it to the class library as a Big Book.

Materials You Will Need

- Favorite class story
- Large chart paper
- Felt-tip markers
- Drawing materials
- Clothesline
- Clothespins

5 Hang-Ups

Clothes hangers are useful for displaying language-experience charts, poems, directions, and other print that your class has generated. Charts expand as a unit progresses and students have additional ideas or information. Hangers allow previously generated charts to remain visible over the length of an instructional unit or longer. Skirt hangers, especially the stacked ones, work well for storage and display.

When the class reads a chapter book, create an attribute web for each of the characters as they are introduced. Hang the attribute webs on individual skirt hangers and display them across the ceiling or along a wall. Have students continue to add attributes to the webs as they read. When they finish the book, have the students work individually or together in small groups to create compare-and-contrast matrices using the attribute webs.

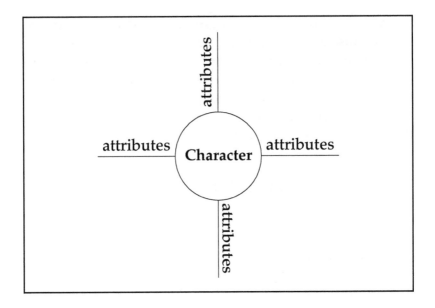

MATERIALS YOU WILL NEED

- Chapter books
- Clothes hangers, preferably skirt hangers
- Clothesline
- Chart paper
- Felt-tip markers

6　Shoe Bag Classification

Classifying, a basic activity for conceptual development, is creating groups of things that are alike in some way, or separating them because they are different. This sorting process is a fundamental thinking skill that students develop by using their expanding experiences and their own language.

Closet shoe bags are an excellent device for categorizing, classifying, and organizing information. Hang them on the back of a door, on the bottom lip of a blackboard, or on a windowsill.

Initiate a brainstorming session with the students to generate a variety of words and short phrases about a given topic. Print these words and phrases on sturdy cards. Elicit at least one idea from each child. Fifty ideas are a minimum; a hundred or more ideas ensure a rich, diverse, creative experience. Have children generate words and short phrases about the following:

- A topic or theme they are studying
- Reactions to a story or an experience
- Observations from a school walk or a field trip
- A current event

Working in pairs or small groups, ask students to sort the cards according to their own classification. Next, have students place the sorted stacks of cards into the pockets of a shoe bag. Label their categories or have other students guess the classification rule for each stack. Learner-centered classrooms value and promote divergent ways of thinking!

As a final step, ask students to re-sort the cards based on different classifications. Having students explain their rationale for sorting, and re-sorting, is an important step in any classification activity.

VARIATION

Another option is to give students the categories for word sorting in order to teach a specific skill or concept. For instance, ask students to sort words based on structural analysis (such as prefixes and suffixes) or based on function (such as animals that live in the woods, on farms, or in the zoo).

MATERIALS YOU WILL NEED

- 100 index cards
- Felt-tip markers
- Shoe bag

7   Word Ribbons

Learning to spell is a developmental process. Learners go through specific stages as they become proficient spellers. According to the National Reading Panel (2000), phonemic awareness supports and accelerates learning to read and spell. Children with greater phonemic awareness are likely to be more successful initially than children who have few or none of these skills. Word ribbons support the development of spelling, phonemic awareness, and phonics skills. Word ribbons immerse students in print and provide specific word selections for children as they continue to explore print.

Word ribbons are long strips of paper on which words are grouped in predetermined categories (e.g., initial or final consonant blend, vowel sound diphthongs or digraphs, rhyming families, pluralization). Word ribbons can be suspended from window shades, door frames, or other infrequently used classroom spaces. They are a quick reference for students looking for a word as well as a launching point for discussion when a child finds a word that fits, or doesn't fit, into a category. Word ribbons are a great tool for the ever-growing collection of language in your classroom.

Initially, word ribbons should be developed with the class during shared reading. After the first read aloud, reread the story and ask students to find words that fit a particular pattern. For example, words that end in –tion, or words that begin with th–. Or they can listen for and look for words with the same letter but with different sounds such as the soft or hard pronunciation of sound represented by the letter C or G. These initial exercises focus on phonemic awareness; they help children notice, think about, and manipulate sounds in spoken language.

List the words on your prepared word ribbons as they are discovered. Post the ribbons so they are visible and accessible to the class to continue adding new examples. As children read and reread the posted lists, they are working with graphophonics; they are learning how to relate letters and sounds together, how to break apart spoken words into sounds, and how to blend sounds to form words. Eventually, students will make these kinds of discoveries about words spontaneously during shared reading or during their individual reading time and request that new word ribbons be created.

MATERIALS YOU WILL NEED

- Favorite read-aloud story
- Long strips of paper
- Felt-tip markers
- Masking tape

8 Class Mailbox

In the learner-centered classroom, students engage in relevant, purposeful reading and writing activities. These tasks engage students in real-life activities and are highly motivating instructional strategies. These activities should include mechanisms that encourage students' writing and provide opportunities for meaningful correspondence. As much as possible, students should have an opportunity to choose what they will write and what format they will use. Provide ample time for writing throughout the school day.

Setting up class mailboxes offers a purposeful opportunity for students to communicate in writing. You can purchase an inexpensive mailbox at a hardware store and decorate it with a montage of students' drawings, theme-based pictures, or each student's handwritten name.

You can also set up individual message boxes for each student. Ask each student to bring in an empty round cardboard oatmeal carton. Discard the box lids and lay each carton on its side. Next, glue the cartons together in a pyramid. (For a class of twenty-one students, begin with a row of six cartons, topped with a row of five, then four, etc.) The result is a "mail-box pod" in which each student has a space where notes can be delivered.

TECHNOLOGY OPTION

Set up electronic pen pals. Allow students to use electronic mail to communicate with students in other classrooms on the campus, or anywhere in the world. When students write for authentic reasons, such as informing others or gathering information or communicating with a variety of other people, their integration of writing conventions improves. When students receive a meaningful response to their writing, the feedback enables them to become more skillful communicators.

MATERIALS YOU WILL NEED

- One standard mailbox or one round oatmeal carton for each student
- Drawing materials
- Glue
- E-mail network

9   Message Center

The Message Center, originated by Carolyn Burke of Indiana University, provides an opportunity for interaction through writing and a purposeful way to develop fluency with written language. Students post messages that inform, persuade, commend, remind, or react. The center encourages sharing ideas, demonstrates the functional nature of writing, and facilitates communication among individuals, small groups, and the whole class. Information, notes, and communications can be posted at the class Message Center. Compliments, invitations, advertisements, and reminders can also be placed at the center.

Create a Message Center by designating a specific area in the classroom where messages can be posted. Choose wall space or an easel with a pad or board. The center should be inviting, attractive, and organized with the appropriate writing and posting materials to facilitate communication.

Write a special greeting or message to your students. In your message, describe the center. Explain what it is and its most appropriate use. For example, discuss and post guidelines for who can use the board, when it can be used, and some of the purposes and logistics of using it (e.g., be sure to include the sender's and receiver's names). Use the center for special announcements such as "It's Joe's birthday today" or "Don't forget about the field trip on Friday" or "Who would like to help clean up the desktops this afternoon?" Students become used to checking the board and anticipating directions and information from the teacher, news of the day from the main office, and personal correspondence from their classmates.

MATERIALS YOU WILL NEED

- Wall space or easel with a large sheet of chart paper
- Felt-tip markers
- 3" × 5" index cards, note paper, or sticky notes
- Masking tape or tacks
- Writing materials

10   Personal Word Banks

Flexibility and choice are important elements in the learner-centered classroom. Rather than create universal spelling lists, encourage your students to keep personal word banks. Students can choose interesting words from shared reading, current-events articles, content area lessons, or from something they have heard on television and would like to learn to spell.

Create word banks by punching holes in index cards and hooking them on a loose-leaf binder ring. They can also be kept in a recipe box, a shoe box, or even a cut-down milk container.

Have students add several words to their word bank each week (the number will depend on the grade level). Students should write each word and illustrate it, use it in a sentence, or both. Provide some time for word bank sharing, either as a whole class, in small groups, or with a partner.

These word bank words become a rich source for vocabulary building. Have students nominate their words with the class voting on words of the week. Ask for nominations and list them on a piece of chart paper or on a section of the blackboard. Have students campaign for their words, or someone else's, by making brief speeches about the merits of the word. After the vocabulary election, list the words of the week on a word ribbon or a visible place in the room. This activity usually leads students to choose intriguing words that are fun to say, complicated to spell, or mysterious in meaning. By creating word banks, the entire class learns many new words that become their own.

Variations

Once the banks contain a dozen words, have students work with a partner to classify or alphabetize the words. They can also use the words to create silly sentences.

Materials You Will Need

- Index cards
- Loose-leaf binders, recipe boxes, shoe boxes, or milk containers

Building on
Students' Experiences

BACKGROUND

Children develop four vocabularies: listening, speaking, reading, and writing. The average five-year-old enters school with a speaking vocabulary of 2,100 words.

Understanding print comes from talking and learning about the world and the written language in it. In the classroom, language learning develops in an environment that is filled with print and offers opportunities for students to use language in purposeful ways. Students need to be immersed in a print-rich environment that relates to and stems from their own experiences. Every classroom should be filled with a wide range of literature, including fiction, nonfiction, and poetry, and a variety of reading materials, such as brochures, magazines, pamphlets, catalogs, and newspapers. Atlases, dictionaries, directories, and thesauruses should also be available. This wealth of materials does not exclude basal readers and textbooks, but the purpose for reading materials should be clear and well thought out. Make materials highly accessible, encouraging students to use them. Once the basic relationships have been taught, the most effective way for children to integrate and extend their knowledge of sound-symbol relationships is through repeated opportunities to read.

Bombarded with print in the environment, students see road signs, theater marquees, storefronts, and advertisements emblazoned with product slogans every day. This environmental print provides the impetus for students to plaster the classroom with writing generated from their own experiences. Some effort is involved in planning and providing for these opportunities, but the accessibility of the materials and the high level of task involvement offer a fair trade-off.

11   Classroom Libraries

According to Routman (2003), classroom libraries are a literacy necessity; they are integral to successful teaching and learning, and a top priority if students are to become thriving, engaged readers. For their reading to improve, students must have access to a great variety of books in every genre and at levels that they can read. The classroom library should reflect the interests of the students in the class and include both classic pieces—such as *Corduroy*, *Where the Wild Things Are*, *Bridge to Teribithia*, and *The Lion, the Witch and the Wardrobe*—and lighter or more contemporary material, including graphic novels, books in a popular series such as the Harry Potter series, and books by popular authors like Judy Blume. Routman (2003) suggests that an adequate classroom library have at least 200 books, and Serafini (2006) recommends 100 books per student!

Build your classroom library by collecting books from every possible resource: bonus points in various book clubs, garage sales, student donations, PTA funding, effective grant writing, and other sources. Most public libraries allow teachers to check out classroom sets, as will many school libraries. Ensure that the collection includes titles from various genres and reflects your students' interests and demographic makeup. It is especially important to include books that the students in your particular class can read independently.

With the students' help, decide on a system for organizing the collection. Use shelving and tubs or baskets to group related books. Grouping options include by author, by series, by topic, or by "what's hot." Many classes keep an "Our Favorites" shelf throughout the year, changing the titles periodically. Use bookstore marketing techniques and, if possible, face the books out so that covers can be easily seen. Students can flip through a plastic tub filled with books facing out much more easily than reading titles on outward-facing spines, especially if the books are paperbacks.

Daily within your instructional day allot at least twenty to forty minutes for students to choose and read books from the classroom library. Many teachers allow students to read wherever they are comfortable, and sometimes in pairs. Options for reading time include the beginning of the day as everyone is arriving, during the day at workstation time, or while the teacher is working with a small group. Early in the year, model how to select an appropriate book, how to treat the book, and how to return the book to the classroom library. Educate parents about the role of the library in your classroom, and oftentimes they will help to make it grow.

MATERIALS YOU WILL NEED

- Books representing all genres
- Shelving
- Storage tubs or baskets
- Labels

12   Mainly Menus

Two key principles of language learning are immersing students in print and providing relevant, meaningful tasks in a real-world context. Familiar experiences and language provide students a foundation for extending language learning.

What better way to connect the two than to collect printed materials from the community and integrate them in the classroom? And the added bonus—you're recycling!

Collect a variety of menus from local restaurants—get multiple copies if you can—and use them to do the following:

- Ask students to choose and illustrate a meal, labeling the items.
- Engage students in role playing with a restaurant scenario. Have them create the setting and write the script.
- Discuss the influence of other cultures on everyday English words. On chart paper, list foreign food words that have become part of our lexicon, such as omelet, croissant, or sauerkraut. You can start a word bank of foreign words and phrases that will be added to throughout the year.
- Do a class/school survey. Create a graph—or several types of graphs—of favorite foods.
- Learn about the food pyramid and create well-balanced menus for the week.
- Create a large Venn diagram on a bulletin board. Have students fill in rings comparing one menu to another based on either the physical characteristics of the menu or the content.

MATERIALS YOU WILL NEED

- Variety of menus
- Drawing materials
- Writing materials
- Chart paper
- Graph paper
- Felt-tip markers

13   Taking Off With Advertising Flyers

Any printed materials with which children are familiar provide meaningful text for literacy development. Oftentimes, even reluctant readers become motivated to read for information and meaning if the content is something they desire such as a new pair of track shoes or the latest release of an electronic game.

Obtain advertising flyers at local supermarkets and discount stores. Flyers offer relevant, current information and support students' connection between school and home. In fact, a good way to involve parents is to ask them to send in flyers they think are unusual or interesting.

Collect multiple copies of advertising flyers and have them available in the classroom. You can use flyers to do the following:

- Develop students' vocabulary. Ask students to cut out a picture that interests them and create attribute webs with the item glued in the center and words describing it extending from the picture.
- Create a class catalog comprised of students' wish-list items. Ask each student to contribute an item and tell a story about why she or he would like to have it.
- Discuss persuasive language, truth in advertising, and consumer bias. Create a wall chart with examples.
- Place copies of grocery store advertisements in the housekeeping center of an early childhood classroom. Encourage students to make a grocery list, complete with items and prices, to do pretend grocery shopping.
- Develop students' ability as discriminating consumers, challenging them to verify claims in an advertisement. Encourage cross-checking of information, using alternate ads, information from the Internet, and human resource specialists.

MATERIALS YOU WILL NEED

- Variety of advertising flyers
- Scissors
- Glue
- Drawing materials
- Writing materials
- Chart paper
- Felt-tip markers

14   Weekly Words

As students explore literature, they can collect and use words that intrigue them to create a word mobile. Once a week, at the designated *mobile time,* have students share the words they've chosen. They can also share definitions, the context in which words were found, or why they think the words are interesting. Have students ask questions or make book recommendations at this time. Suspend the mobile from the ceiling above the students' desks or in another area of the room, school library, or hallway. As students complete their mobiles, they fill the classroom with print.

Have students identify words they find interesting or unusual. Instruct them to use markers or crayons to write their words on one side of precut paper (6" × 2") and their name on another. Save these strips until the class fills its mobile.

Create the mobile in advance and fill it in during the month, one side each week. To construct a square-shaped mobile, do the following:

1. Fold a strip of tagboard (24½" × 3") into four six-inch sides. Staple the ends together.

2. Use the extra half inch to create two one-quarter-inch tabs for stapling.

3. From the center of each side of the mobile, staple a piece of construction paper (12" × 2½") for hanging the students' chosen words.

4. Glue the words of the week onto each side of the mobile until it's completed.

To hang mobiles, staple one piece of yarn or string to each corner and tie them together at the top. Mobiles can be suspended from the ceiling above each student's desk. Provide a string and hook that stay in the ceiling so the mobiles can be removed and replaced easily.

MATERIALS YOU WILL NEED

- Felt-tip markers or crayons
- Precut 6" × 2" strips of paper
- 24½" × 3" tagboard or oaktag strips
- Stapler
- Construction paper
- Yarn or string
- Hooks
- Glue

15   The Living Bulletin Board

As responsibility is nurtured in the classroom, students assume many tasks that were once reserved for the teacher. Creating and contributing to a class bulletin board is one way that students can increase ownership in their classroom. A living bulletin board is a section of the classroom where a story is illustrated or a concept is depicted. The board continues to grow as the students' knowledge about a particular topic, concept, or unit develops. This creative display involves the entire class and presents an authentic demonstration of the groups' increasing understanding. This visual expression of printed material enhances students' understanding and cultivates their imaginations.

Students can use a living bulletin board to review information or jog their memories.

As students begin reading, discussing, and learning about a new topic, they create a scenario, or living bulletin board, that is expanded and enhanced as their knowledge and understanding grows. The living bulletin board is a class project; design ideas should come from students. After you explain the nature of the bulletin board and decide on a topic, ask the class to brainstorm ideas for figures and scenes to get started. Cover an unused bulletin board or wall space with white paper and divide it into several sections or scenes.

This organic display comprises people or characters with dialogue bubbles. Scenes should be labeled and captioned. Have students work in groups to develop layout, create figures and scenes, and decide about dialogue and captions. Figures and structures are added and dialogue and captions are modified as the unit progresses. As choices are made determining the bulletin board format and content, the opportunity for collaborative planning and decision making among students is enhanced.

Materials You Will Need

- Large sheets of white paper
- Drawing materials
- Writing materials
- Tacks, staples
- Scissors

Establishing
Literacy Workstations

A literate life is carefully constructed . . . by creating classrooms in which reading is a constant daily presence. Independent reading is a context within which children can see themselves as readers and build habits that can last a lifetime.

—Gay Su Fountas and Irene Pinnell

BACKGROUND

In a learner-centered classroom, teachers purposefully plan to ensure that students function independently, participating in authentic literacy-building tasks and events. One way to encourage a variety of literacy behaviors and to enable a teacher to focus attention on one student or a small group of children is the establishment of literacy workstations.

A workstation is a designated area in the classroom where materials, supplies, equipment, and often students' work related to a particular content area, skill, or activity are organized. Workstations, or centers, can be permanent and related to an activity or subject area, such as a publishing center or a math area. Workstations can also be flexible and temporary, organized around special interests, themes, or units being studied. Try building a station around familiar and popular reading materials such as Harry Potter or Dora the Explorer books.

Literacy workstations offer opportunities for self-directed learning and provide a stimulating environment in which students exercise and reinforce skills and discover and explore new topics. Workstations promote student choice and provide an opportunity for students to develop responsibility and self-reliance. Many learner-centered teachers allow their students to help organize and develop the stations in the beginning weeks of school. Including students in the design of their classroom builds a sense of pride and community and helps develop the housekeeping skills necessary to maintain a busy student-centered classroom. Students should have some choice in developing ground rules for their center-based activities. Choices include which workstations to visit, length of visit, and which activities to complete. An agreement can be reached among the students that determines how many and which activities are required during a day, week, or unit; which activities are optional; and which are free choice.

Workstations can be carved out of unusual or out-of-the-way places in the classroom: a tabletop, a bookshelf, in a corner, or even space beneath a table. It is important not to place traditional seat-work kinds of activities in various places around the room and call this a "workstation." Effective stations are filled with hands-on, authentic tasks, often using self-correcting materials. For rich literacy development, listening, speaking, reading, and writing stations should be included in your classroom.

16 Workstation Rules

Clear expectations and consistent routines support children's growing independence. It is important to inform students about the purposes of each station and discuss rules that will ensure its best and most productive use. Students are more likely to understand and follow rules when they help organize and develop them.

Develop rules for each workstation and for workstations in general. Begin with teacher modeling of appropriate and inappropriate behaviors at each workstation. Through whole-group discussion, generate a list of rules connected to these behaviors, and create charts and other visual displays (drawings, photographs, posters, etc.). Post the rules at each station. Many teachers use the phrase *at this station, I can . . .* and then list all appropriate behaviors. Use the input from the students about what they think appropriate workstation behavior should be.

Use print and rebus writing for beginning readers. Reinforce the rules as part of the collaborative classroom.

MATERIALS YOU WILL NEED

- Chart or construction paper
- Illustrations
- Drawing materials
- Tape

17   The Key to Knowledge

Children are quite self-reliant when they work within a consistent structure. They learn to respect rules that are clearly established and reinforced. Sometimes workstations are a free-choice activity. Other times they are a scheduled part of each student's day. Either way, some method of monitoring traffic—who goes where, when, and for how long—must be established.

One management method is to color code each workstation to make it easily identifiable. For example, the listening station is red, the writing station blue. Create a number of tagboard keys in corresponding colors.

For primary students, hang keys on long pieces of yarn, enough for students to wear as necklaces. For older students, create a Key Pass in each color. These are the keys to the various workstations. When stations are free choice, students choose a key and enter the station. For scheduled visits, students take the assigned key and do the same. The keys enable you to scan the class to be sure everyone is in the proper place.

Limiting the number of keys to a station allows you to control the size of the group. Add or take away keys when stations or station activities change. Hang the keys on hooks or pegs in an accessible spot.

MATERIALS YOU WILL NEED

- Tagboard or construction paper
- Yarn
- Hooks or pegs

18 Housekeeping

A child's sense of inclusion in the classroom community is a prerequisite to academic success. By giving students classroom management and record-keeping tasks, you are contributing to their sense of responsibility to and membership in the classroom.

You can make students part of the workstation monitoring routine, free a bit of your time for instructional tasks, and decorate the classroom. Creating cardboard houses that indicate when a student is "in" is one unique way to allow students to track their own attendance.

Construct tagboard houses to represent each literacy workstation. Attach houses to a bulletin board or wall at the front of the classroom for easy access. Divide the area into sections for each workstation. Simple house shapes will do, or create dwellings from a certain geographic region or historical era, a certain novel or story, or the houses of well-known authors. Cut slits in each window of the house to form a pocket. The number of pockets should equal the number of students that can comfortably work at the station simultaneously. Have students create name cards using index cards. They can color one side green and the other side red. Prereaders can use photos of themselves as well as write their name on a card. Assign students to a station by placing their name card in the window, green side up. When students have completed their work at the station, they can turn their card to the red side. This will help you keep track of their progress.

Materials You Will Need

- Tagboard
- Felt-tip markers or crayons
- Index cards
- Photos for prereaders
- Glue
- Scissors

19   Introducing the Writing Workstation

A hallmark of the learner-centered classroom is its writing and publishing center. In these classrooms, writing goes on continuously. The writing workstation is filled with accessible materials for writing, illustrating, and creating a finished product for "publication." It also contains many models of the conventions of writing, such as enlarged letter forms, samples, and rules for punctuation and grammar, and reference resources like dictionaries, thesauruses, books of quotations, and zip code books.

Early in the school year, introduce the students to the writing and publishing center. Allow them to practice writing while sitting on the floor using clipboards, lap desks, and slates. Show the children how to store these portable surfaces in a large plastic bin or on pegboard hooks for easy retrieval and return. With the students, brainstorm ways to keep the writing materials organized and easy to reach. Model these organizing methods, as well as how to use the pencil sharpener and three-hole punch stored in the workstation.

Have the students select samples of their best writing to be kept in the writing station. These samples can include stories, poems, advertisements, articles, letters, greeting card messages, banners, fact sheets, memos, notes, flyers, and schedules. Students can develop classroom posters illustrating the conventions of language and display the posters near the writing station. Additionally, teacher-made charts with convention examples (e.g., commas in a series) should be available. Encourage the students to display magazines and newspapers on skirt hangers or to sort them into colored bins.

As students publish their own writing, add these works to the writing station. It is important for students to see their writing published and shared with others. Publishing guidelines should be established so students feel secure with the process and understand that it is achievable. Published work should demonstrate high standards. More information on writing stations is found in Section 3, "Developing Fluent Comprehension."

MATERIALS YOU WILL NEED

- Clipboards, lap desks, slates
- Large plastic bins or pegboard hooks
- Pencil sharpener
- Three-hole punch
- Writing samples
- Writing materials
- Drawing materials
- Skirt hangers

SECTION 2

Orchestrating Student Interaction

As we come to understand that meaning is socially constructed and context-dependent, we realize that learning must involve collaboration—collaboration between students and teachers, between students and published authors, between writers and readers, and among students themselves.

—Judith Newman

A fundamental assumption about learning emerging from the current research in cognitive science indicates that learning is the act of constructing knowledge, and that exploration and discovery is most effective when students have the opportunity to build knowledge with others. When students talk with each other, they are encouraged to think out loud, clarify ideas and thoughts, and vocalize new terminology. A related assumption is that human beings produce, share, and transform knowledge singly and in groups. Learning is enhanced when students are engaged with others in the classroom community. They benefit from the variety of social contexts that are possible within a classroom community: whole-group, small-group, and individual instruction (Fountas & Pinnell, 2006).

Knowledge is a cultural artifact that is distributed among members of a group. When knowledge expands in this manner, the knowledge of the group becomes greater than the knowledge of any single member. In learner-centered classrooms, engaging and authentic tasks done in small groups allow students to make connections, develop concepts, and better understand themselves and their world through the exploration of literature and content area printed materials.

Buddy Studies

Learning in Pairs

BACKGROUND

During their formative years, children develop speech patterns and usage conventions based on exposure to the language around them. Language and language use are determined by social situations. Language development involves collaboration in the negotiation of meaning. By participating in conversation, children further develop their understanding of language. Children use the linguistic resources available to them to make meaning of their experiences and build the semantic and syntactic forms through which that meaning is expressed. Reading, writing, and sharing with others become tools for making discoveries about the world.

Children require partners to become proficient at listening and speaking. Establishing a learning environment where children consider each other as resources and recognize that we are smarter together than anyone is alone encourages the social information processing necessary for language learning.

Harvey and Goudvis (2007) suggest that the number one thing that enhances comprehension is to talk about what one is learning. Simple, interactive configurations can be structured to provide opportunities for students to share and discuss information without major changes in instructional methods. These opportunities provide welcome breaks in the routine. They also allow students to construct personal meaning from new concepts. By structuring opportunities for students to *turn and talk*, teachers enhance information processing and conceptual understanding. Partnered interactions balance participation and reduce the potential for the most vocal students to dominate the learning environment.

The National Reading Panel (2000) points out that cooperative or collaborative learning has been used effectively to teach comprehension strategies in content-area subjects. As students work as partners, applying strategies to understand content-area text materials, they support each other's learning.

20　Turn to Your Neighbor and . . .

Thinking aloud with someone else promotes clarity in thinking. Students can be paired in various ways throughout the school day and year. Pairs configured for quick tasks and changed frequently add variety and multiple perspectives to students' thinking.

You can pair students by using proximity (turn to the person on your right, behind you, to the east, etc.) as a simple and quick method to reinforce those concepts.

After a read aloud or shared reading experience, ask students to turn to their neighbor to discuss new information. To help recall the discussion, younger students can use paper and pencil to draw or jot down their partners' thoughts. Some possibilities include having students do the following:

- Explain or clarify a particular passage or event
- Generate several adjectives for one of the characters

- Discuss the author's use of setting, plot, theme
- Answer a specific directed question

With consistent use, students become familiar with this *think/pair/share* structure, and it is rarely necessary to reinforce the appropriate behaviors.

VARIATION

Partners report: Tell the class that you will select several students to share their partners' ideas. In this way, students are accountable to each other and to you for providing some information.

MATERIALS YOU WILL NEED

- Read-aloud literature
- Writing materials

21 Level-of-Learning Reading Partners

In addition to independent reading time, students benefit from reading with a partner on a regular basis. In this particular learning-buddy structure, partners are formed based on similar achievement level and remain together for an extended period. Achievement-alike partners operate on the premise that pairs can read the same books and that the likelihood that a strong reader doing most of the work is reduced (Calkins, 2001).

Paired work is enhanced when students are taught to question and prompt one another. Clear, consistent teacher modeling of these skills is an effective way to transmit these skills.

Level-of-learning reading partners share the decision about how they'll read their book. Options include the following:

- Choral reading: One of the readers introduces the book to the other. Holding the book between them, they do a choral reading.
- Alternating reading: After choosing their book, partners take turns, each reading a few pages aloud and then switching.
- Echo reading: One partner reads a chunk of pages aloud. Then the other rereads the same text. (This option is especially effective with emergent readers).
- Skit reading: If there are characters and dialogue in the book (*Frog and Toad, Pinky and Rex, George and Martha*), partners may choose to take parts and act out the story.
- Read and discuss: For chapter books (e.g., the *Henry and Mudge* series), partners can each read a chapter individually, noting sections or passages they wish to discuss with their partner. Discussion time can be structured for balanced participation so each reader has a chance to lead the conversation.

MATERIALS YOU WILL NEED

- Appropriately leveled texts
- Partner assignments

22   Learning Partners

In contrast to quick pairs, learning partners stay together for a designated period: a week, a marking period, a full school year. Establishing learning partners among your students is an effective way to build trust; partner students for paired activities; and build listening, social, and metacognitive skills.

Have students choose their learning partners, or randomly or strategically assign partners based on achievement level, social skill, or gender. When random groups are desired, partners can be formed by:

- Student lineups: Students form a line by birthdays (or other criteria) and count off pairs to create learning partners.
- Card matching: Distribute cards with authors and titles and have students find their match.
- Random selection: Form pairs by allowing students to mill about. Call "Stop!" and direct them to face the person closest to them.

Direct learning partners to choose a specific spot in the room where they will meet whenever a learning-partner activity is announced. Learning partners can be paired for any of the partnered strategies in this book.

Use learning partners to promote student thinking. Ask your students to meet with their partners to do the following:

- Make predictions about a story or book they are about to hear or read
- Think about reactions to a shared reading, a current event, a hypothesis
- Respond to a metacognitive stem written either on the chalkboard, chart paper, a smartboard, a PowerPoint slide, or on paper for each student; some examples include

  The most significant thing I learned about was . . .
  I want to be sure to remember . . .
  Something I would do differently next time would be . . .

MATERIALS YOU WILL NEED

- Various forms of literature and reading materials
- Chalkboard, chart paper, or media
- Writing materials

23   Paired Verbal Fluency

Constructing language and listening to the ideas of others prepares students for further instruction by stimulating thinking. It also increases students' preinstruction knowledge base and clarifies any misconceptions they may be bringing to the lesson. Paired verbal fluency (PVF) can be used to activate students' prior knowledge and experience before holding a class discussion, or as an effective prewriting activity.

Choose partners and have each pair decide who will be Person 1 and Person 2. Students will alternate speaking in three rounds of various lengths.

During the discussion, partners must listen carefully to each other without interruptions. They are not allowed to repeat anything they or their partner has already said. Students should rely on their memory instead of using their notes.

At your signal, Person 1 begins. After the selected time elapses, Person 2 takes over. The rounds go as follows:

- First round: 60 seconds each
- Second round: 45 second each
- Third round: 30 seconds each

Lengthen or shorten the length of each round to suit the dynamics of the class, grade level appropriateness, and content discussed.

Finally, as a whole class or in a grouping of several partners, students record their ideas and information on chart paper for sharing and discussing. They can save ideas for later use as well.

Paired verbal fluency is also a good closure activity. After students have listened to a story, taken a field trip, or participated in a lesson, ask them to do a PVF.

MATERIALS YOU WILL NEED

- Chart paper
- Felt-tip markers

24   Learning-Partner Biographies

In learner-centered classrooms, each student is a learner and a teacher. Giving students an opportunity to learn about each other helps them learn about other cultures, explore different family lifestyles, and consider new hobbies and interests. This experience also begins an important first step in understanding and being understood by others.

Students need to see themselves as individuals, as well as part of a larger social and cultural group.

Learning-partner biographies is a twist on the more traditional assignment of writing an autobiography at the beginning of the year. Learning-partner biographies is an effective strategy to use early in a learning partnership. Students create (or are given) interview questions to ask their partners. Based on their interviews, students write about their partner's life or some aspect of it. Younger students can illustrate an important time in their partner's life or some of their partner's favorite things.

MATERIALS YOU WILL NEED

- Interview questions
- Writing materials
- Drawing materials

25   Summary Pairs

Far too often, when reading silently, students pay too little attention to the text. Readers must be taught to have an *inner conversation* as they read, monitoring their comprehension, identifying what they do and do not yet understand. When readers need to explain what and how they understand to others, it makes them more likely to apply, extend, and simplify that information. Responses to reading can be expressed in writing or demonstrated through creative dramatics or drawing. In this case, the responses are verbal summaries. Summarizing a piece of reading gives students an opportunity to evaluate the piece, consider the author's intention, and make connections to their own experiences.

Summary pairs alternate reading aloud and summarizing paragraphs (or any other predetermined section). Students can choose the length of the passage they will read; however, pairs need to agree.

One student reads aloud and then summarizes what has just been read. The second student adds anything that was left out, emphasizes key points, or even offers comments about the content.

Both students must agree on the significant points before continuing. The process is repeated with the second student reading aloud. Partners alternate in this manner until the selection is completed.

MATERIALS YOU WILL NEED

- Various literature or subject area text for oral reading

26   The King and Queen of Questions

For an effective classroom community, children must believe that they are contributing and that their thoughts are worthwhile. With this strategy, the King and Queen of Questions are selected students who consult with other students needing assistance. In this way, students don't stay stuck; they recognize each other as resources and realize that the adults in the room are not the only sources of knowledge, information, or answers. Because everyone eventually gets a chance to be the expert, and because peers are continually assisting peers, all students develop self-reliance and problem-solving skills when a classroom incorporates a King and Queen of Questions.

Familiarize students with the King and Queen of Questions in your classroom as early in the school year as possible. Explain to the students that the king and queen serve as leaders in problem solving; they are not expected to generate answers or know the solutions. Their task is to suggest problem-solving strategies. They might brainstorm possibilities, generate alternatives, or offer possible resources.

The role of the king and queen rotates among class members daily, weekly, or in time frames you deem appropriate. The monarchs are not chosen based on academic ability. An equitable rotation system should be established so all students are aware they will have a turn. Consider organizing pairs with different strengths and abilities to enrich everyone's learning opportunities.

Every student should have an opportunity to be king or queen because every student has the capacity to be thoughtful and strategic. However, you might want to begin with students who have strong social and problem-solving skills to present an appropriate model and establish high expectations.

Structuring Small Groups

Background

Working creatively and cooperatively as a team member requires skills that current competitive jobs require. Working cooperatively in small groups at school offers great benefits to students. They are more likely to be successful at a wider variety of learning tasks; they increase their problem-solving and decision-making capacities by sharing strategies with others; they are more articulate and clearer in their verbal expression as well as their thinking; and they increase their positive feelings about themselves and school in general. However, to reap these benefits, small-group work must be highly structured, and group processes must be taught and reinforced.

Johnson and Johnson (1988) describe five elements, or conditions, of cooperative learning: positive interdependence (sink or swim together), face-to-face interaction (to promote each other's success), individual and group accountability (no hitchhiking, no social loafing), interpersonal and small-group skills, and group-processing skills. In cooperative learning structures, each member of a team is responsible not only for learning what is taught but also for helping teammates learn, creating an atmosphere of achievement. Students work through the assignment until all group members successfully understand and complete it. At the conclusion of any task, the group-processing phase is critically important, as team members discuss how well they have achieved their goals, how effective their working relationships have been, and if any changes in group behavior are merited to secure improved results.

27   Story Map Trios

Story structure describes the way the content events of a story are organized into a plot. Being able to recognize story structure increases students' appreciation, understanding, and retention of stories. As students read various genres of literature, they begin to understand that different types of written work follow specific maps. For example, a typical plot profile for a short story would have a beginning problem (or problems), a series of scenes leading toward a resolution, a climactic event (or denouement), and an ending. Students should become familiar with these story maps to become fluent readers and better writers.

During this activity, students read material aloud together or read silently to themselves. Then, in groups of three, students develop a story map on paper and identify key elements of the plot. To foster positive interdependence, assign the following roles to group members:

- The cartographer: The cartographer captures the group's thinking and records it on the story map. If the group decides to brainstorm a number of possibilities, the cartographer should record these. However, the cartographer must wait to be sure everyone agrees before filling in the story map.
- The navigator: The navigator makes sure that all members understand, agree, and are comfortable with the group's decisions. The navigator guides the group work, steering its efforts through any problems and making sure everyone is included and contributing to the group's efforts.
- The explorer: The explorer works to extend the group's thinking by exploring all avenues of thought. The explorer might ask questions like, are there any other important events we haven't considered? What other possibilities are there? Where can we look for more ideas?

- Short stories
- Writing materials

28   Get the Point

Consensus building requires students to articulate individual points of view and listen with empathy. These important skills support students in learning to use conflict constructively. When consensus is the goal, students must engage in dialogue and generate a plan, a statement, a conclusion, or ideas with which they all agree. This process aids students in clarifying and articulating their own points of view, developing active listening skills, building effective group-process skills, and broadening individual perspectives.

To get the point, students read a chapter aloud and then individually write what they think are the most important points of the passage. Working in groups of three, students each have one minute to present their points. The group must agree on and be prepared to share at least three significant points from the selection with the full class. They must be ready to justify their choices based on the story. A facilitator, who ensures the group's completion of the task in a timely manner; an arbitrator, who checks for understanding and agreement; and a secretary, who records the group's work, help to structure group productivity. When it's time to share, a reporter for each group should be chosen randomly. This ensures that all members contribute and understand and share the group's thinking.

Extend this activity by bringing the whole class together to create a class list of the most significant events in the chapter. List the events on large chart paper. Have students add to the list as they read subsequent chapters. Use the list as the basis for a discussion of theme, tone, author's purpose, and other points. Process the group work by analyzing the various group-work techniques that were used to help each group reach consensus.

MATERIALS YOU WILL NEED

- Reading material
- Writing material
- Large chart paper
- Felt-tip markers

29   Peer Revision: Learning Together

Students need to assess a piece of writing based on both their own internal criteria and their own external established standards for quality. Students develop and exercise this ability by assessing their writing and the writing of others. Further, an effective peer-revision process develops students' academic and social skills. The process of peer revisions begins with whole-class work and moves to structured pairs.

WHOLE-CLASS WORK

Start by having the whole class analyze a piece of writing, noting strengths and weaknesses. Then, have the class develop the criteria for a quality piece of written work, generating a list of characteristics of good writing. Next, have them work in small groups to apply these criteria to samples of published works. Ask students to substantiate their evaluations with specific references to the work. Then have them apply these criteria to samples of students' work from previous years, other classes, or other grade levels. Finally, ask the groups to apply the criteria to samples from their own class.

PAIRED WORK

Establish revision partners. If working in pairs is new to the class, have partners do several interactive tasks that are low risk to build their relationship (see "Buddy Studies: Learning in Pairs" for ideas). When students begin this process, focus their attention on a particular purpose for each editing session. During one session, students might look for clear transitions between sections and the use of details to support main ideas. In the next session, they may look for mechanics and word usage. Be sure to establish operating ground rules for editing partners. Some suggestions:

- Base your feedback on the agreed-upon criteria. Be as specific as possible.
- Monitor time and use it wisely. Take turns so each partner has time to consider the work and offer support.
- Be an active listener. Paraphrase and clarify responses to communicate your interest and understanding.

MATERIALS YOU WILL NEED

- Writing samples or students' work
- Colored pens or pencils for editing and revising

30 Peer Editing: Sharing Glows and Grows

Students often discover strengths and weaknesses in their own writing by reviewing a partner's writing. Having the opportunity to read the work of other students helps all writers increase their own vocabulary, style choice, and topic ideas as well. Sharing praises and goals—a colleague in

Arkansas calls them *glows and grows*—sends the message that each piece of work has merit and that everyone can identify goals for improvement. Sharing praises and goals pushes students to go beyond a polite positive response or a damaging negative one. It forces them to be thoughtful and specific in their critiques.

Before students engage independently in glows and grows, be sure to model the language and intentions of an effective peer-editing comment. Then, using a piece of your own writing, let students generate a few glows and a few grows for you to be sure they're ready for independent partnered work.

Students review their partner's work, identifying several things that worked well and several things that could be improved. At the peer-revision sessions, students must be prepared to do the following:

- Provide at least two praises for things that were strong in the work
- Offer two suggestions for development or improvement

Note: Editing control remains with the author at all times.

MATERIALS YOU WILL NEED

- Students' work
- Colored pens or pencils for editing and revising

Reading Conference

Flexible Student Grouping

BACKGROUND

Reading groups have been a long-held tradition in elementary classrooms. In most cases, reading instruction occurs in small groups of students with similar abilities. Children are aware of their perceived status as readers no matter what clever names are assigned to their reading group. Call them vultures or eagles, students know which group is "smart" and which is not.

In theory, grouping students according to their abilities is designed to help teachers provide the most appropriate pacing, materials, and instruction for all students. In reality, however, children placed in low-ability groups are at a disadvantage. In fact, the bottom group in one school may be of equal ability to the top group in another. However, students placed in the bottom group may perceive themselves as poor readers, and their teachers may have lower expectations for their achievement. Due to these perceptions, as well as qualitatively different instruction among levels of groups, the initial group designation can become a self-fulfilling prophecy. The methods of assessing reading ability, and concurrently for placing students in reading groups, are unreliable and fallible. Yet once students have been placed in a group, it is very difficult for them to switch. Some researchers believe that a young child's success as a reader is determined not by ability but by the reading group into which the child is initially placed.

In learner-centered classrooms, student groups are flexible. The teacher is a mediator of instruction, structuring opportunities for students to work together and facilitating their process. As students function at a high level of engagement with information and with each other, teachers have more freedom to interact with all groups and to check in with students in one-on-one conferences. Small groups may be organized around specific strategies that the teacher wants to introduce or reinforce. The composition of the groups changes as students gain mastery or require support. Small groups are also organized according to common interests in a particular topic, genres of literature, or authors.

A reading conference is a formal opportunity for these small groups to meet with the teacher. The composition of the conference group may change based on the selection students are reading or students' specific needs and interests. The reading conference is generally conducted with small groups of students, although individual student conferences can be scheduled as well.

31 Establishing the Climate

A literature-based reading conference provides an opportunity for young readers to experience literature through interaction with others. Students support each other when they make meaning of what they read and connect it to their lives. The climate of the reading conference must be supportive and comfortable.

During the reading conference, teachers have an opportunity to shape students' development and positively influence future reading selections. Conference discussions are designed to promote divergent thinking. Learners understand that their responses are valued and will be given due consideration. Students have the opportunity to discuss, explain, consider new possibilities, change their minds, and engage in speculation.

Conduct the reading conference in a comfortable spot in your classroom, such as a conference table or carpeted area. It is important to arrange the seating so there is eye contact among participants.

Involve students in establishing the psychological climate by explaining your purposes, what you hope to accomplish, and the importance of the conference. Let students have as much input in establishing the environment for the conference as possible. Ask them what kinds of supplies are important to have and what kinds of behaviors and attitudes are important to bring to the reading conference. List appropriate behaviors on chart paper and post in the reading conference area.

Decorate the conference area with students' artwork; ask them to create illustrations of their favorite stories or bring quotes from their favorite authors to personalize the display.

MATERIALS YOU WILL NEED

- Chart paper
- Felt-tip markers
- Drawing materials
- Writing materials

32   Student Preparation

A reading conference allows students to share reactions and feelings about a reading selection, hear others' points of view, clarify misconceptions or confusions about the text, extend real-life experiences by discussing related topics or issues, and make plans for further reading. Students should have these purposes in mind when preparing for a conference. Reading conferences help students develop responsibility for their own learning and thinking. Many students are unfamiliar with reading conferences and will need support in preparing for them. Being prepared creates a confident, able learner.

To assist students in preparing for their first few conferences, you might require them to do one or more of the following:

- Be ready with a selection to share
- Bring a written reaction to the text, perhaps a page from their reading journal
- Bring an illustration of a scene, character, or event
- Generate several questions or things they are wondering about regarding the story
- Share something they have in common with a character or an event in the plot
- Prepare a critique of the book

Materials You Will Need

- Copies of the reading selection

33   Temperature Checking

The reading conference provides an opportunity for monitoring student development, or *temperature checking*, touching base with students individually and assessing their academic progress. The conference is a forum where students ask questions, consider multiple perspectives, make connections to their own experiences, discover themes, and deepen their understanding and appreciation of literature. Small-group reading conferences help students understand that interpretations of and responses to the same piece of writing can be varied.

Reading conferences can serve as a short cycle assessment when scheduled specifically as an opportunity to gauge students' progress with their reading and determine whether some intervention or assistance is necessary. For this purpose, create a regular schedule with the same groups of students. For example, if you have twenty-five students, you may want to see five each day. These conferences are usually short and occur at regular intervals. They provide a time-efficient method to maintain regular interaction with each student. During the conference, check that learners are progressing comfortably, sustaining their chosen directions, and continuing to be challenged.

A scheduled conference is a time to review reading folders before each session and make appropriate notations during or after your interactions. (See more on assessment in Section 5.)

MATERIALS YOU WILL NEED

- Record-keeping sheet for each student
- Student reading folders

34   Developing the Format

To establish an environment where students are willing to speculate, take risks, and personalize their reading experiences, model these behaviors yourself. During the reading conference, show your own love and enthusiasm for reading. Share your reasons for reading, favorite places to read, how you choose what to read, what you do after you read—everything about your reading life! Be a colearner by sharing your views on a piece of literature and demonstrating your processing by thinking aloud with the students. With younger or beginning readers, the conference provides an additional opportunity for modeling book handling, directionality, and using illustrations to predict and comprehend.

By maintaining a consistent conference format, children know what to expect and can anticipate the nature of the discussion, thereby enabling them to feel more secure.

Although there is no one way to conduct a reading conference with a group of children, an effective conference format will include the following:

- Discuss the reading material as a whole. Listen to children's responses, suggesting they summarize the story or retell a particular scene or event. Model how to paraphrase and clarify responses.
- Ask the students both literal and inferential questions about the text, and have them ask questions of each other. Learner-centered classrooms promote divergent thinking, so encourage personal connections to the reading to be shared aloud.
- You may wish to require students to read portions of the text orally. The purpose of oral reading should always be connected to content, related to understanding, or for the genuine pleasure of the language.
- Discuss goal setting with the students. Ask students what they plan to read next and why. They should leave the reading conference with these next steps in mind.

MATERIALS YOU WILL NEED

- Paper
- Pencil
- Prepared questions
- Students' current reading selections

35 Flexible Groupings

There are multiple purposes for holding small-group reading conferences. Students can gather to discuss their reading progress based on a variety of formats and functions. A conference can be held to discuss and consider specific elements of literature, a particular author, a common theme or interest, or other topics. Multiple-purpose groupings allow you to monitor student progress while allowing for flexibility and choice.

Decide on a purpose and a grouping strategy for your reading conference. Here are a few possibilities.

LITERATURE LEAGUES

Groups for a reading conference can be based on various organizing factors. Some possibilities include students who have been reading the same book, different books by the same author, different books with similar themes, or different books within the same genre.

SPECIAL INTEREST GROUPS

Special interest groups (SIGs) can be formed based on students' interest in topics or types of literature. SIGs can be formed around a book series, like the Alex Rider books or Artemis Fowl series, the Judy Moody books, or Ron Roy mysteries. SIG groups can be scheduled for an hour every Friday and attendance rotated throughout the month.

SKILL AND STRATEGY INSTRUCTION

Groups can also be assembled based on identified needs or interests. You may want to assign a reading selection and direct the questions and discussion to a specific instructional purpose such as characterization, inferencing, phonics, or application of thinking strategies. With younger children or less proficient readers, conduct the conference while the reading is taking place. This format is referred to as *guided reading instruction,* where groups are pulled together for a specific and usually temporary purpose. See Section 3, "Developing Fluent Comprehension."

36   Working One on One

There are a number of reasons for conducting individual reading conferences. They provide rich and direct attention to an individual child. They offer a close evaluation of individual progress and help address any immediate concerns. Individual conferences may be important for students who need additional help or are not yet confident in a small-group setting. They can be initiated by you or the student and can be scheduled regularly or conducted intermittently.

When you feel a student needs close, individual attention, schedule a one-on-one reading conference. Calkins (2001) distinguishes among three different types of individual interaction: conferencing, coaching, partnering.

- Conferencing: The intention of a one-to-one conference is to evaluate where each child is as a reader, inform individual and small group goal setting, and begin/continue the process of supporting literacy development.
- Coaching: Imagine running alongside an athlete interjecting brief bits of advice, and you have the idea of what a coaching conference might entail.
- Partnering: When partnering, the teacher engages with each child at a level just beyond the student's independent level, hoping to raise the child's level through apprenticeship.

A one-to-one conference may focus on one or a combination of all three approaches.

Maintain an individual student conference log to record the date of each conference, with space for comments. Remark on student's developing attitudes, skills, and knowledge. Combine the conference log with other record-keeping devices to establish a holistic picture of each student's progress. (For more on assessment, see Section 5.)

MATERIALS YOU WILL NEED

- Record-keeping sheet for each student

SECTION 3

Developing Fluent Comprehension

Children need to learn letters, sounds, words, sentences, and how to comprehend what they read simultaneously.
—Ellin Oliver Keene

When my daughter was three, we moved from one town to another and were involved in packing our house. We had been particularly busy wrapping our fragile things when we ran out of boxes. On the errand for additional packing materials, we passed a hardware store with the word "GLASS" in the window in large neon letters. Happily, my daughter pointed and exclaimed, "That's the store where we got our boxes. We can get some more boxes there." When I asked her what made her think so, she replied, "That's what it says on our boxes at home!" She knew, through her own experiences, that boxes from a particular store often have the store's name printed on them. She had seen the label "GLASS" on the boxes at home filled with breakables. Thus she inferred from that experience that the boxes came from that store and that we could get more. —L. L.

Children expect print to carry meaning that relates to a situation. Even before they can officially "read," children readily use knowledge of their environment to make sense of print. They sort through their prior experiences and apply what they believe to be relevant knowledge. Language offers three primary sources of information, or cueing, systems: semantic, syntactic, and graphophonic. Semantics relates to connotation of words and the meaning we make from language. Syntax relates to the grammatical arrangement of words and the rules governing those arrangements. Graphophonics involves the sound-symbol relationship of language. It includes both the visual representation of language—such as letters, spelling patterns, punctuation, spacing—and the phonemic, or sound, system. These semantic, syntactic, and graphophonic cueing systems are used in concert with experiential knowledge to discern and create meaning while reading, writing, listening, and speaking.

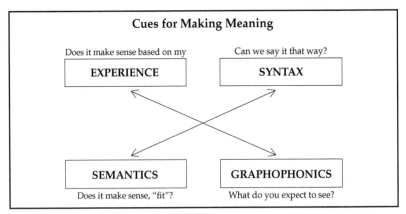

Cues for Making Meaning

Does it make sense based on my	Can we say it that way?
EXPERIENCE	**SYNTAX**
SEMANTICS	**GRAPHOPHONICS**
Does it make sense, "fit"?	What do you expect to see?

Reading is a process of predicting, confirming, and integrating information. Skilled readers use these cueing systems interactively to cross-reference and confirm their predictions and the meaning they are making from the text.

This cross-checking can raise discrepancies and facilitate self-correction and confirmation. Thus it is important that students have facility and flexibility with all three sources of information without being overly dependent on any one. Proficient readers monitor and regulate themselves. They recognize when meaning has been lost and have strategies for regaining understanding.

The National Reading Panel (2000) has identified fluency as a key component of effective reading. Fluency is the ability to read with speed, accuracy, and proper expression with automaticity, that is, without conscious attention.

Current research on proficient readers has confirmed the power of comprehension-strategy instruction to enhance fluency. Specific and explicit instruction in comprehension strategies promotes the active nature of the reading process in students (Keene & Zimmermann, 2007). Findings by the National Panel on Reading suggest that the comprehension strategies found to be most effective include the following:

- Comprehension monitoring, or metacognition: Strategic readers are able to think about their own thinking, identifying what to do when they don't know and choosing from an array of potential next steps.
- Cooperative learning: When students listen to and speak with each other, sharing their thinking and considering the ideas of others related to what they are reading, they increase their individual repertoire of reading strategies and their own comprehension abilities.
- Graphic organizers: Visual or graphic organizers—such as semantic webs, paragraph frames, and story maps— illustrate concepts and the interrelationships between concepts in a text. These visual representations increase focus and allow readers to examine text more fully. They also provide an effective bridge for written expression.
- Story structure: Story maps, timelines, plot diagrams, character attribute webs allow students to surface the elements of literature for examination, discussion, and further study.

- Question answering and question generating: Focused questions, posed either by the teacher or by the students, give students a purpose for reading and increase comprehension skill. Questions can be *text explicit* (literal), *text implicit* (inferential), or *scriptal* (based on the students prior knowledge and experience).
- Summarization: Summarizing requires readers to identify what is important in a text and then use their own words to succinctly convey these ideas. Summarization-strategy instruction supports readers in understanding main idea and supportive detail, connecting interrelated ideas in text and retention of printed material.

These strategies are most effectively learned when applied in authentic contexts as a blended approach. That is, the teacher might model an approach to comprehending text using several strategies and sharing the what, why, and how of the combined strategies being used. A balance of explicit instruction and blended application launches students on a lifetime of skillful reading.

Developing Skills by Increasing Fluency

When fluent readers read silently, they recognize words automatically. The group works quickly to help them gain meaning from what they read. Fluent readers read aloud effortlessly and with expression. Their reading sounds natural, as if they are speaking. Readers who have not yet developed fluency read slowly, word by word. Their oral reading is choppy and plodding. Fluency is important because it provides a bridge between word recognition and comprehension.

—National Reading Panel

BACKGROUND

Because I travel a great deal, my daughter Vanessa has learned some vocabulary associated with packing. In our house, we've labeled cosmetics, shampoos, and other essential toiletries. Of course, when we leave home we pack our toiletry bags. Once, when she was about six, she was in her room with a friend getting ready for a sleepover, and I heard uncontrollable giggling. Curious, I went into her room only to see Vanessa laughing hysterically and her poor friend with a totally confused expression. As it turns out, Vanessa had explained that she was almost ready—she only had to pack her toiletries. Her poor confused friend was in a quandary, trying to picture what a "toilet tree" would look like—and why she would need to bring it! —L. L.

Children use what they know about the world and connect what they know about language to make meaning. From their initial encounters with language, they develop a semantic and syntactic sensibility. They use these cueing systems, along with their previous experiences, to understand text. Fluent readers continually confirm predictions and generate new ones. They confirm or refine tentative understandings based on additional information, integrating new information and using it as a basis for further predictions. Students who do not develop reading fluency, regardless of how bright they are, are likely to remain poor readers throughout their lives.

37   Choosing and Using Predictable Text

So much of the literature we love is built on predictable patterns. These patterns help emerging readers read independently by making educated guesses about the text. Research has shown most children's sense of story structure develops very quickly. By the time children who have had experiences with stories enter school, they have a surprisingly sophisticated understanding of characterization, plot, and setting. Knowledge of story structure enables readers to identify key information and remember important elements. Stories that conform to a good story structure support students' capacity to make meaning from text, as does a good match between text and illustrations.

To help students make predictions based on text patterns, choose a book with a predictable pattern to read aloud. Some patterns to look for in choosing predictable text include the following:

- Repetitive patterns organized by repetitive language or episodes (e.g., *The Gingerbread Man*)

- Cumulative patterns where stories continually add and repeat events that have occurred previously (e.g., *The Little Red Hen*)
- Interlocking patterns where the portion of a previous page will be incorporated into the following one (e.g., *Brown Bear, Brown Bear*)
- Chronological patterns, which follow a time sequence or cycle (e.g., *The Giving Tree*)
- Familiar cultural patterns, which are based on patterns such as the alphabet, days of the week, or months of the year (e.g., *Chicken Soup with Rice*)
- Rhyme/rhythm patterns where rhyme or rhythm is built into the text, sometimes found in nonsense stories (e.g., *The Cat in the Hat*)

Periodically, stop reading and allow the children to predict what will happen next. Children will naturally begin choral reading as they predict the next patterned occurrence. Allow them to chime in as you read.

MATERIALS YOU WILL NEED

- Large selection of read-aloud books containing predictable patterns

38   Innovations on Text

Both semantic and syntactical knowledge are used strategically to derive and create meaning in reading, writing, listening, and speaking. Creatively playing with predictable patterns, or innovating on text, is an effective strategy for developing students' capacity for using semantic and syntactic cues.

Conduct a shared reading or read aloud a book or poem that has a predictable pattern. Invite students to develop their own stories using the fundamental patterns and elements of the original story while incorporating their own creative changes in the text. Here are some ideas:

- Change the main character. For example, in the charming book by Laura J. Numeroff, *If You Give a Mouse a Cookie*, students can change the mouse to another animal or to a person to create some interesting plot twists. Examples include *If You Give a Horse a Carrot* and *If You Give Your Mom a Hug*.
- Change the setting. Imagine if Goldilocks were a mermaid and the story took place under the ocean instead of the woods.
- Change the plot. Add a new ending, additional chapter, or an epilogue.
- Change the format. Turn a short story into a poem or a biography; turn a fairy tale into a newspaper article.
- Change the perspective. Write the story from the protagonist's or minor character's perspective. For example, what would *Three Little Pigs* be like from the wolf's perspective?

MATERIALS YOU WILL NEED

- Book or poem containing a predictable pattern
- Writing materials

39   Toot! Toot!

Shared reading is one way of immersing students in rich literary language without concern about grade level or reading performance. Make use of the patterns found in songs, poems, and nursery rhymes to develop syntactic and semantic strategies. Text innovation based on playground chants, nursery rhymes, holiday songs, familiar camp songs, and even rap music can be used in the classroom for creating interest, involvement, and humor. *Toot! Toot!* is a good example of this genre.

Place the following chant on a large chart paper, an overhead transparency, or in a pocket chart. Increase the speed of the reading as you proceed. After choral reading, distribute worksheets with blanks, as follows:

Toot! Toot!

A peanut sat on a railroad track,
His heart was all a flutter,
Along came engine number 9
Toot! Toot!, peanut butter!

Toot! Toot!

A _____ sat on a railroad track,

_____

Along came engine number 9

Toot! Toot! _____!

Have students work in pairs or small groups to generate their own chants. Ask students to prepare their chants on charts or sentence strips to share with the class. Here is an example to get them started:

Toot! Toot!

A *lemon* sat on a railroad track,
Trying to get some shade,
Along came engine number 9
Toot! Toot!, *lemonade!*

As each group shares its chant, the class reads with them. It's fun to encourage the class to try to predict the final line. Post the finished products around the room to add to the print-rich environment and offer additional reading practice opportunities for the students.

MATERIALS YOU WILL NEED

- Large chart paper, overhead projector, or pocket chart with sentence strips
- Worksheets with fill-in-the-blank chant for each student
- Writing materials

40 Radio Reading

Having students read the same text repeatedly is an effective instructional method for increasing fluency. Interestingly, research has shown that repeated oral readings lead to improvements in reading not only the familiar passage but also of passages students have not previously seen. Repeated reading helps readers recall facts from their reading, helps them remember important information, leads to improved story comprehension and more sophisticated questioning, and promotes faster reading with greater word recognition accuracy (Rasinski, 2003).

The problem is that rereading for its own sake can be dull and tedious. To increase motivation and still achieve the benefits of repeated reading, try *radio reading*.

For radio reading, gather a group of four to six students. Choose a passage that students can read with 85 percent to 95 percent accuracy and assign a part to each student the day before the radio read. Note: with any repeated reading strategy, teachers must be familiar with common target reading rates. Hasbrouck and Tindal (2006) offer the rates shown in the box on the next page. It is effective to choose a text that the group has already read silently. Give a mini-lesson on the importance of reading with meaningful expression, just as radio and television announcers do. Remind students that the only way to read with such expression is through practice.

Grade	Words Per Minute
1	80
2	90
3	110
4	140
5	160
6	180

Regularly listen to students read appropriate leveled text, noting their reading rates. This requires a stopwatch and a record-keeping system of noting how many words per minute the student reads correctly, including self-corrections after errors. For students reading below the expected reading rates, employ the following strategies.

Allow time for the students to practice their parts, individually and cooperatively. Ask each student to prepare two questions based on her or his portion of the text. One question should be literal and one inferential. On the following day, have students meet as the group and present their parts (with expression!) one by one, in appropriate order. You can provide a microphone prop to help make the experience more authentic! After everyone has read, encourage the students to discuss their questions, summarize the reading, critique their performance, and make suggestions for the next radio reading.

MATERIALS YOU WILL NEED

- Appropriately chosen text
- Microphone or karaoke machine as a prop (if desired)

41 Say It Like the Character

Oral reading fluency means more than reading accurately and quickly. It also involves reading with expression, appropriate pace, and *prosody* (phrasing). Some children read accurately but continue to read word by word because they do not break text into proper phrases (prosody) or use expression as they read. As a result, comprehension breaks down. In Say It Like the Character, students are instructed to consider the tone of the passage, as well as what the character is saying.

Choose a passage that contains monologues or dialogues. If the text is unfamiliar to the students, give them background information so they will understand the context of the spotlighted portion. Provide a copy of the text to each child. Have them practice reading the text silently and orally. Next, read aloud a portion of the text in several tones of voice (angry, sad, delighted, surprised) and talk about the feelings that can be inferred from your expression.

Once students understand the process, have them try Say It Like the Character on their own with a new passage. Assign them a feeling to embed in their reading (or let them choose a feeling), and have them practice reading their passage to perform it for the class. During the performances, have the listening students guess which feeling the reader is trying to convey.

MATERIALS YOU WILL NEED

- Passages with monologues or dialogues
- Emotion cards

42   Reader's Theater

Reader's Theater simultaneously gives students an opportunity to enjoy meaningful children's literature and participate in effective reading practice Reader's Theater improves student interest and confidence in reading, as well as overall fluency in the number of words read correctly per minute. Unlike traditional round-robin reading, where students often count sentences ahead and nervously await their turn, Reader's

Theater offers readers "the opportunity to become familiar in advance with the text they will read, to practice it until they are fluent with it, and then to relish the positive experience of reading that well-practiced text aloud for an audience" (Buzzeo, 2006). Like a play, Reader's Theater involves scripts to read, but that's where the comparison ends. There is no memorization involved, nor are there costumes, props, or sets. Reader's Theater yields improvements in students' word recognition, fluency, and comprehension.

Acquire or create a script based on quality children's literature. To create your own, adapt the text of a favorite book. Use stories with interesting characters, lively dialogue, and interesting problems. Remember to include narrators.

For ready-made scripts, consult Buzzeo (2006) and the following Web sites:

http://www.aaronshep.com/rt

http://www.readers-theatre.com

http://www.geocities.com/EnchantedForest/Tower/3235

http://www.storycart.com

http://www.readinglady.com

http://www.lisablau.com

Read the book or story upon which the script is based aloud to the students. Discuss the illustrations, the meaning of the story, and other elements.

Conduct a mini-lesson based on some aspect of fluency, for example, phrasing, reading like a character, or verbal expression.

Distribute photocopied scripts to all readers and determine parts. It is helpful to provide two copies each so readers can take one home for additional practice. You might divide several parts to include more student readers. Those without speaking parts will be the audience and have their turn with a future story.

Allow the readers to practice reading; provide advice and support as needed, choosing coaches from students without speaking parts.

For the performance, have the readers face the audience and simply read their parts in turn. Celebrate the quality reading that has taken place.

MATERIALS YOU WILL NEED

- Children's literature/trade books
- Scripts

43 Partners Predict

Partners Predict is a strategy for reading aloud that incorporates both prediction making and cooperative learning. Partners Predict enhances speaking and listening skills, as well as reading comprehension. Adding the cooperative element of student interaction increases both motivation and learning. This strategy enhances the read-aloud experience by keeping students actively engaged with each other and the material.

Organize students into pairs before a shared reading. Begin by reading the title of the selection or the genre of literature. Have partners predict what the story might be about. For example, if the selection is a fairy tale, ask students to predict what they might find in the tale (magical characters, wizards, a princess, etc.). Then, periodically stop reading and ask partners to predict what might happen next. Listen to a few of the predictions and then continue the story. Students love to listen to see whether their predictions were correct.

MATERIALS YOU WILL NEED

- Read-aloud book or poem

44 Opin

Debate and discussion of word meaning and nuance help students connect prior knowledge and experience with text meaning. Discussing shades of word meanings allows students to discover the importance of context and the value of their own experiences in comprehending written material. Most vocabulary is learned indirectly, but there is a place for direct vocabulary instruction in a learner-centered classroom.

Opin is a motivating activity that generates interest in a piece of literature (or content-area material) while developing vocabulary and comprehension fluency. Originally developed by Frank Green of McGill University in Montreal, opin incorporates writing, speaking, and listening experiences by requiring students to predict, clarify, debate, and discuss word meanings within a context.

For each student, photocopy a segment of a story and replace ten to twelve words with blank spaces. Delete words that have many possible synonyms. Read the story to the class. Stop when you get to the opin section, and distribute the photocopies.

Step 1: Students complete the opin sheet individually, filling in each blank with an appropriate word.

Step 2: In pairs, students compare their responses and attempt to convince their partners that their word choices are best. They must justify their claims based on the text. Students can change and refine their work or add an answer if they did not have one. Partners may even decide to generate a third choice.

Step 3: Lead a class discussion by asking, "How many of you had answers that differed from your partner's choice?" Almost every hand will go up! "How many of you changed or modified your responses based on your discussion?" Elicit a few examples and discuss them. Ask, "How many of you are curious about the author's choices?"

Step 4: Read the conclusion of the story and ask students to compare their responses to the original text. Stress that the author's choices are not the correct answers.

To adapt opin for primary students, retype or enlarge the text so students have room to fill in the blanks. To increase attention to graphophonic cues, the teacher may choose to fill in the initial letter of the blank words to narrow the scope of possible responses.

MATERIALS YOU WILL NEED

- Opin exercise sheets for each student
- Writing materials

45 Word Splash

The National Reading Panel Report (2000) confirmed that teaching specific words before reading helps both vocabulary learning and reading comprehension. *Word splash* is a powerful prereading strategy that exercises prediction-making skills, provides a contextual definition for vocabulary students encounter in reading, and increases students' motivation to read.

Word splash is adapted from a strategy called *key word*, originally developed by reading researcher Dorsey Hammond of Oakland University in Rochester, Michigan.

A word splash is a collection of key terms or concepts selected from a reading selection, chapter in a textbook, or audiovisual materials students are about to read, see, or hear. The selected terms are written at odd angles splashed on a chart or overhead transparency. Another option is to give groups or individuals copies of the splash on which to record their statements. Working in pairs or small groups, students generate complete statements—not just words or phrases— that predict how the words might be used or what the selection might be about. Roles can be assigned to students, for example, recorder, reader, checker.

Once the ideas are generated, students are given the reading selection or other information. They read it together and pause at appropriate spots to check their predictions against the text presented. Students should modify their statements as needed and place a question mark next to any unclear statements.

MATERIALS YOU WILL NEED

- Overhead projector or easel with chart paper
- Felt-tip markers
- Photocopies of word splash sheets
- Writing materials

46   Say Something

Fluent readers integrate semantic, syntactic, and experiential knowledge in order to predict, confirm, and interpret text. Students need to feel comfortable reading unfamiliar words and integrating the complex ideas and information they are reading. Harste, Short, and Burke (1988) originated this interactive strategy for developing students' confidence and ability to focus on meaning rather than on print when reading. This strategy helps students develop a relationship between what they are reading and what they already know.

Students work as partners, each with a copy of a reading selection. Before reading, students decide how they will read (silently or orally, in unison or alternately) and how far they will read before stopping to react. Students then read, stopping at the predetermined point—a paragraph, a page, or a chapter—to *say something*. The *something* can be a question they might have, a reaction, a description, information from either their own experiences or other sources that is confirming or contradictory. You may want to assign specific reactions or provide pairs with a list of possible *somethings*.

After each pair of students has completed reading and discussing the selection, they share insights and interpretations with other pairs or individually write a journal entry.

MATERIALS YOU WILL NEED

- A reading selection for each student
- Journals
- Writing materials

Extending the
Reading Experience

Reading demands a two-pronged attack. It involves cracking the alphabetic code to determine the words and thinking about those words to construct meaning.
—Stephanie Harvey

BACKGROUND

The world's store of knowledge doubled and doubled again during the twentieth century. A weekly edition of the *New York Times* contains more information than the average person in seventeenth-century England was likely to encounter in his or her lifetime. A National Endowment for the Arts survey, *Reading at Risk: A Survey of Literary Reading in America* (2004), reported that fewer than half of American adults read literature. Their study describes an alarming decline in the reading of literature between 1982 and 2002, with the steepest rate of decline, 28 percent, occurring in the youngest age groups. Electronic media, including the Internet, video games, and portable digital devices, have increasingly drawn Americans away from reading books. The number of Americans who say they've even opened a single book of fiction, let alone a poem or a play, over the course of a year declined from an already low 56.9 percent in 1982 to 46.7 percent in 2002.

The National Assessment of Educational Progress (National Center for Education Statistics, 2000) national reading assessment of fourth-grade students found that 87 percent of students who reported reading for fun on their own time once a month or more performed at the proficient level, whereas students who never or rarely read for fun performed at the basic level. Students who read for fun every day scored the highest. However, beyond test scores as a measure of success, if we are to be a literate society, we must encourage students to recognize that reading is a satisfying personal experience, a quest for information, and a way of connecting with the world.

47   Figures of Speech

The English language is filled with idioms. Idioms are figures of speech that carry meaning not explicitly stated in words. Idiomatic expressions are complex and can be difficult for students to understand, particularly young students and students for whom English is a second language. Many idioms in English have analogous but not exact translations in other languages. For example, the English expression *pulling my leg* means the same as *tomando el pelo* in Spanish, which translates literally as "pulling my hair." By working with idioms in our classroom, we encourage students to infer, a key skill used by proficient readers.

Generate a class list of idioms. Body parts, common animals, and various foods are sources for many idiomatic expressions in the English language.

Some examples include *it's raining cats and dogs, you're pulling my leg, I'm so hungry I could eat a horse,* and *you look like a million dollars.*

Students can do this task in a number of ways, including working with partners in small groups or individually. Have students review literature and identify idioms in class or assign as homework.

Once you have a list of twelve to fifteen idioms, ask students to illustrate the literal meanings of the expressions. Post these in the classroom or make a class book. Discuss why these illustrations are humorous. Contrast the literal and idiomatic meanings of the illustrations. How are idioms useful in helping us express ourselves and understand our world?

MATERIALS YOU WILL NEED

- Writing materials
- Drawing materials

EXTENSION

Use the idioms and illustrations created in Figures of Speech, or specific idioms identified by students in their reading, to invent stories that explain how a particular idiom developed. Illustrate and share these "myths" as a class publication, bulletin board, or hallway display.

48   Create a Comic

One way to allow children to exercise their imagination is by creating something funny. A sense of humor is a sign of intelligence and can be developed in the classroom. The familiar structure of comic strips offers a great way to develop children's senses of humor, as well as their reading and writing fluency.

Comic books are a frequent reading choice for students who grow up to be fluent readers.

The enticing visual cues and simple sentences of comic books give the struggling young reader "training wheels" while developing proficiency. Comics require readers to infer meaning from the pictures and few words.

Survey the class for favorite comic strips and comic-strip characters. Encourage students to bring in their favorites from the Sunday paper and provide a forum for sharing. During whole-group lessons, analyze the comics, discuss what makes each one funny. Use a *think aloud* to model the process that you (as a proficient reader) use to understand the comic.

After students have had success with understanding the comics, ask them to create their own. This can be done by copying the full strip and leaving the final block blank for students to create their own ending, or by copying the full strip and leaving all the bubbles blank for students to fill in their own dialogue.

EXTENSION

Have students create their own comic strips based on class or school activities and people. Create class comic books by developing familiar characters of your own.

MATERIALS YOU WILL NEED

- Comic strip samples
- Photocopies of samples with blocked areas
- Writing materials
- Drawing materials

49 Finding Common Ground

Several studies indicate that using instructional time to build background knowledge increases reading comprehension. Miller (2002) refers to using one's background knowledge as "using your schema." Surfacing students' own experience as it relates to the content allows for the important text-to-self and self-to-text connections critical for skillful reading. These individual reference points are also a rich resource for collaborative conversations

In learner-centered classrooms, students are regarded as independent thinkers who influence and are influenced by the larger learning community. Each student is a complex individual identity. Opportunities for students to share their thoughts and consider others' perspectives support this message. For this purpose, respectful disagreements appreciating multiple points of view and consensus building are important skills.

Finding Common Ground can be used to explore controversial issues based on social studies content, current events, health topics, or life in school or at home. Ask students to discuss an assigned issue with a partner through loosely structured interviewing. When they find something they have in common, they say "OK" and stop. Students each take a few minutes to write down reflections about the interaction and areas of agreement and disagreement. Then students take turns reading what they've written, clarifying and refining. Finally, the pairs synthesize their reflections into several paragraphs to submit to the teacher or read to the class.

MATERIALS YOU WILL NEED

- Writing materials

Integrating Instruction

On a recent visit to a second grade classroom in upstate New York, a life-sized poster of an armored knight greeted me at the door. I saw schematics of castles, a large wall mural illustrating a medieval scene with royalty and serfs, knights and horses, and a semantic web on the board with vocabulary and ideas from Marguerite de Angeli's *The Door in the Wall*. On the daily calendar, each date was written inside a little turret, and the name tags on each student's desk read "Princess Susan" or "Prince Raoul." The class was enthusiastic and informed me that they had been learning about medieval times, architecture, social structure, and folk legends and literature. The thematic unit had evolved from a piece of text about a young knight and sparked children's natural interests. —L. L.

BACKGROUND

In real life, content area distinctions blur and disciplines overlap. Children should not have to be their own curriculum coordinators. When teachers organize instruction through integrated thematic units, students see the connections between subjects and subject areas and become more involved with the multiple aspects of the information they are learning. Skills, knowledge, and attitudes are reinforced within and across disciplines. Integrated instruction makes better use of instructional time and provides a deeper look into subjects through a variety of content-specific lenses. When students have the opportunity to work with multiple sources of information, they gain a more inclusive perspective than they would from consulting one textbook (Wood, 1997).

When curriculum is set in the context of authentic human experience, its relevance to real-life learning becomes clearer for students. Integrated instruction emphasizes content knowledge and understanding in relation to broader issues and perspectives. Integrating information and connecting content areas increases the likelihood of learners making connections and drawing relationships of their own.

50   Student-Selected Theme Topics

One of the most common forms of curriculum integration is the thematic unit. Themes range from ecology to homelessness to the universe. Teachers select themes based on content mandated for their grade level and available instructional materials. Integration does not negate basic skills. An integrated approach provides a real-world context for developing literacy and numeracy.

Themes ignite student learning especially when the students are involved in selecting them. Student-selected themes ensure relevant learning. Once students see the connection between things they are using in life, learning at school becomes purposeful and meaningful.

Lead your class through a brainstorm session of topics to study. Ask the students what local and global issues they are interested in, and record their ideas on chart paper or smartboard. Examples may include energy consumption, public housing, gun control, homelessness, pollution, and animal rights. As the group discusses the topics, suggest combinations of related ideas to make each topic more comprehensive. When at least twenty to thirty ideas have been generated, allow students to vote and narrow down the list until consensus is reached.

Once a topic has been selected, determine what the students already know and what they would like to learn about it. Make a two-column class chart, listing what the students know on the left side and questions they have on the right. Help students form teams to study particular questions about the topic. Use the two-column chart to guide your integrated instruction.

MATERIALS YOU WILL NEED

- Chart paper or smartboard
- Felt-tip markers

51   Civic Projects

In life, a variety of skills and knowledge is applied toward working successfully in a variety of contexts. We don't view the world in subject-matter fragments, yet we often organize the instructional day in discrete packets of discipline-oriented time. One way for students to experience an integrated, interdisciplinary curriculum is to involve them in a service project in their community. A civic project synthesizes learning from various disciplines and shows students that learning is applicable in the real world.

Generate student interest in a civic project by reading aloud a newspaper article about someone providing service to another person or group. Consider with your students the wide range of projects they could perform in their own community. Discuss ideas such as community beautification, crime fighting, the environment, health, the elderly, literacy, politics, and safety. Allow students to collaborate on and propose a specific project to the class. Following class discussion, use a voting system to decide which civic project will be undertaken.

To accomplish the civic project, everyone must research the topic, using books, articles, interviews, community records, electronic media, and videos. Student committees should be established to define goals, set schedules, estimate costs, consider the needs and availability of the recipients, create advertising, and gather needed materials. During the project, students should capture the event with note taking and video/audio taping. After the project, encourage students to reflect on their experience through discussion, writing, drama, and artwork. Analyze the kinds of skills and strategies the students have used throughout the project, and design further instructional activities based on data and learning gained from the experience. *The Kid's Guide to Service Projects* by Lewis (1995) is a great resource for finding ideas.

TECHNOLOGY OPTION

Encourage students to present their findings in a PowerPoint slide show or with MovieMaker. Invite other classes in for the presentation, celebrating both the service provided through the project and the information literacy skills exhibited through use of the technology!

MATERIALS YOU WILL NEED

- Newspaper article about a person providing service to another person or group
- Reference materials and resources
- Writing materials
- Video or audio equipment

52   Imagine If You Were . . .

Effective curriculum integration centers on a theme that blurs the boundaries among subject areas and focuses on the development of important skills and attitudes. This approach to learning offers opportunities for highly engaging, innovative instructional activities. Among the possibilities are projects, problem-based learning, and action research. In each of these areas, simulations that capture students' imaginations and have real-life application are powerful instructional tools for an interdisciplinary approach.

Role scenarios allow students to gain multiple perspectives on an issue, explore interesting professions, and apply critical skills for lifelong learning. They also allow students to engage in complex problem solving. Students apply their critical and creative thinking to nonstructured problems they encounter outside of class.

Using role scenarios in your learner-centered classroom allows students to exercise their imaginations, work individually or with teammates, and choose a role or area of study they find intriguing. Ask students to imagine themselves in a particular role. Then have them solve a problem or complete a specific task or project from the perspective of that role. Following are some examples of roles.

MUSEUM CURATOR

- Describe, create, or illustrate an exhibit.
- Decide what items to include and why.

ADVERTISING AGENCY DIRECTOR

- Review a piece of advertising for bias.
- Create a marketing campaign and develop promotional materials.
- Design a book jacket or a movie poster.

Tour Organizer

- Design travel or cultural guides within specific contexts or parameters, such as an architectural tour in the year 2165.

Psychologist/Sociologist

- Develop a survey and create a visual or graphic display of the results.
- Draw conclusions to present to the class.

Archaeologist/Anthropologist

- Review information such as a video clip, artifact, or description for clues regarding culture, time frame, and social context or purpose.
- Collect artifacts and create their story.
- Compose essays on essential questions such as, what is the meaning of life?

Newspaper Editor or Journalist

- Write a publication during a specific historical period.
- Write an easy-to-understand article on a complex subject.
- Write editorials or opinions from multiple perspectives.

Historian

- Analyze controversial accounts of historical events.
- Interview others to compose an oral history.
- Write a bibliographic essay that presents an analysis and synthesis of three different sources on the same topic, event, or theme.
- Design a meaningful textbook and create an outline or table of contents.
- Predict a future event based on a past event.

Personnel Director

- Create interview questions.
- Develop criteria for a quality employee, productive team member, excellent student.

Teacher

- Develop a meaningful lesson plan.
- Describe how you would teach a complex topic, sequence of events, specific operation, or solution to groups with varying characteristics or special circumstances.

Expert Witness

- Give testimony to a congressional panel or grand jury about a specific historical event.

Play or Movie Director

- Give a character analysis and stage directions for a specific scene in a play.

Scout Leader

- Create requirements for a new merit badge, such as the Ideal Sixth-Grade Student or the Expert Problem Solver.

Materials You Will Need

- Writing materials
- Drawing materials

SECTION 4

Nurturing Lifelong Learners

Literary reading in America is not only declining rapidly among all groups, but the rate of decline has accelerated, especially among the young ones.
—Reading at Risk: A Survey of Literary Reading in America, National Endowment for the Arts

My first teaching job was with a class of ungraded six- and seven-year-olds in a residential setting with very few resources. It was important to me to provide my students with varied experiences in an atmosphere of safety and comfort and to be an excellent scavenger. At the time, I was living in a cabin on a lake. One day I discovered an irreparable hole in the bottom of our rowboat. Turning bad luck to good, I installed the boat in the corner of my classroom. Filled with pillows, it became a choice spot for quiet independent reading time. Above the boat, strung across the wall, was an old fishing net decorated with bright letters that read "Get Hooked on a Book." Splashed across the net were colorful cardboard fish—small yellow guppies, larger red barracuda, and big blue sharks. After a book conference, students "filled out" a guppy with the name of the book, the author, and the illustrator and hooked it on the net. Ten guppies could be exchanged for a barracuda and five barracuda for a big blue shark. Even though there were various accolades and privileges for increasing the number of books read, being a shark was considered a special accomplishment. Each month, the reading sharks got to have lunch with the principal!

Years later, while standing in a line at Disney World, a young man approached me and introduced himself as a former Big Blue Shark from all those years ago. Today, he is an elementary school principal who reads aloud to each class regularly. As teachers, the time, energy, and love we invest can yield unexpected windfalls. —L. L.

When Calkins (2001) describes her desire for all of her students to be lifelong readers, she puts it into very practical terms. She tells her students' parents, "You can hold me accountable for [your children] bringing books on trips, reading during vacations, and asking for magazine subscriptions for birthday presents. You can judge my teaching by whether [they] initiate reading in their own lives, whether they weave books into their lives with the people they know and the passions they feel." In a learner-centered classroom, teachers help children want the life of a reader and help them to envision that life for themselves.

Routines for Reading to, With, and by Children

Few children learn to love books by themselves.
Someone has to lure them into the wonderful world of
the written word; someone has to show them the way.
—Orville Prescott

BACKGROUND

A well-balanced literacy-development program includes reading to children, reading with children, and reading by children. Reading out loud to children helps them develop a love for good literature, motivation to pursue reading on their own, and familiarity with a variety of genres. Listening comprehension comes before reading comprehension. The listening vocabulary is the reservoir of words that feeds the reading vocabulary pool. We introduce three times as many rare words when we read aloud to a child or during sustained silent reading than we do in conversation. (Rare words are those not found in the most commonly used 10,000 words.)

The best choices for read alouds are books, poems, and stories that you love yourself. Your enthusiasm and joy will come through as you share the work with your students and enjoy it once again through their eyes. When reading *to* children, we open up a world in text that would otherwise be unattainable to them.

Like reading aloud, shared reading motivates children, provides a common experience with a text, and requires no special grouping of classmates. During shared reading, students view the text and follow along with what is being read by the teacher in front of them. Beyond appreciation for the written word and exposure to print materials, shared reading teaches verbal expression and models fluency in reading. It also motivates students to increase their own independent reading skills.

Guided reading is an effective routine for reading *by* children. During guided reading, students are flexibly grouped according to a specific need or developmental level. The format of the guided reading lesson depends on the developmental level of the group, which might range from emergent to fluent. Instruction focuses on increasing students' capacities to solve problems presented by text, using one or a combination of semantic, syntactic, or graphophonic cueing systems (see Section 3, "Developing Comprehension Fluency"). After small-group instruction by the teacher, students have the opportunity to practice the new learning on text that is appropriate for them.

53   Read Alouds

Reading aloud serves a variety of important purposes. Reading aloud inspires interest and curiosity. It engages children as explorers—entertaining, informing, and explaining the world around them (Trelease, 2006). Although there is increased emphasis on explicit reading comprehension instruction, it is still critical that *read alouds*—pure reading to children for the sheer pleasure of it—are built into the daily schedule. Expose students to different genres by reading aloud from a wide variety of material.

When reading aloud, you are the expert reader in the classroom, modeling for twenty-some apprentices just what reading is all about. Choose text that you love, emphasize fluent reading behaviors, and don't be afraid to show how emotionally intense a piece of writing can be.

Students never outgrow the usefulness or enjoyment of listening to read alouds; this routine should occur daily across the grade levels. This relatively simple routine serves to improve comprehension and vocabulary, increase fluency, and build motivation in your students.

Choose a read aloud that interests students. Books that connect with what you are studying provide an extra bonus. For example, Laura Ingalls Wilder's *Little House* books are perfect read alouds in most fifth grade classrooms that are studying westward expansion. For younger students, choose a book that can be completed in one sitting. For older students, read a little each day from a chapter book. The selection should appeal to you and model the conventions of language and good literature.

Set the scene by sharing the title, cover illustration, and something about the author or setting. Then read the text, showing the illustrations and the text itself whenever possible.

Don't be surprised if your learners seek out their own copies of the story to read and reread on their own!

MATERIALS YOU WILL NEED

- Quality pieces of text in which you are interested

54 Familiarity Breeds Confidence: Shared Reading

Just as with a bedtime story, shared reading allows students to revisit familiar literature and discover new adventures in a warm and supportive environment. Start with simple rhymes, songs, and poems that may already be part of the children's repertoire. Remember that exposure to a variety of literary genres prepares students to be more fluent readers and writers. Occasionally allowing the class to choose the book for sharing includes them in the experience. Shared reading experiences demonstrate and reinforce reading as both pleasurable and meaningful.

In shared reading, the students see the text, listen as the teacher (expert) reads it with fluency and expression, and are invited to join in. Use a Big Book, a piece of chart paper with the text written on it, or a transparency containing the text as your resource. Poems are especially effective because they are complete selections with frequently smaller amounts of print. As you read, emphasize your expression and engagement with the text. Invite the students to join in, perhaps on the second reading. Many teachers use the same piece of text all week, thereby enabling even the most reluctant readers to join in confidently by the end of the week. The teacher can demonstrate any reading behaviors and highlight skills during a shared reading experience: fluency, the author's craft, how to decode unfamiliar words, characterization, how to read nonfiction, connecting self to text and text to self, and reading for the pure pleasure of it.

As the students join in, occasionally use oral cloze (pause in your reading so that they may provide a word or complete a sentence without support). After reading the text, encourage students to discuss with partners something about the text so that a focus on meaning is maintained throughout the lesson.

MATERIALS YOU WILL NEED

- Books, poems, and stories of various genres in a format visible to the students

55   We Are Readers: A Class Record

Experience with a variety of literature and other reading materials is important for developing readers and writers. As students accumulate reading experience, it is beneficial to document this achievement. When students keep track of their own growing list of readings, a record exists that can reveal preferences, gaps in reading experiences, and consistent choices. Even more important, learners have a tangible record of accomplishment. Reading logs help students set goals for their literacy learning.

A class list of readings, displayed prominently, allows students to share recommendations and seek out others who have similar reading preferences. This type of record helps determine special groups, activities, and enrichment for your class.

Keep a growing list of titles of books read by individuals and by the class. Class lists can be general or categorized in a number of ways:

- Genre of literature
- Interest groups
- Author or illustrator

Post the lists on large chart paper. These charts help connect students who have read the same titles or are interested in recommendations. The charts also display the amount and variety of reading material that has been consumed—so students can see they are indeed readers. No matter how the list is categorized, include the title, author, class ranking of the book (three stars, smiley face, thumbs down, etc.), and the genre. One classroom I visited had a chart called We Recommend, and individual students were allowed to add titles and reasons for recommendation to the list. Another nice variation, especially in a primary classroom, is to include the book cover next to the title of the book on the chart. This helps young readers remember which book was which, and encourages text-to-text connections during all reading experiences. Find book cover images on Web sites such as www.bn.com or www.amazon.com; download, print, and post.

MATERIALS YOU WILL NEED

- Individual lists for each student
- Large chart paper
- Felt-tip markers

56   Sustained Silent Reading

The premise of sustained silent reading (SSR) is a simple one: Students need an opportunity to independently exercise their newly developed skills. Using SSR is just as simple; students choose something to read and spend time and attention reading it. First introduced in the early 1960s by Lyman C. Hunt Jr., a professor at the University of Vermont, SSR increases the amount of time students spend with books. SSR can also develop dramatic changes in reading ability and, perhaps more important, in positive attitudes toward reading. The one thing that makes the biggest difference in students' reading performance is spending extensive periods every day actually reading (Keene & Zimmermann, 2007).

To institute a sustained silent reading program, you will need to consistently devote time each day for everyone in the class to spend time reading a book of choice.

Here are a few important tips for a successful program:

- Begin with a limited amount of sustained reading time. Approximately ten minutes to begin is an appropriate amount. Increase the time in small increments, until primary students are reading for twenty to thirty minutes at a time, and intermediate students are reading for forty to sixty minutes per session.
- Allow students free choice in their reading materials, and do not connect any assignments or reports to this reading. Ensure, however, that the books are readable

by the child. Children who continually practice with materials that are too hard for them will not make gains in reading.

- Once students have selected their reading materials, they must quietly sit and read. Students cannot change books during SSR time. Primary students should have a book bag with five or six appropriate titles inside so they will not run out of reading material. Many teachers choose Monday as the day to "shop for books" in the classroom library, when students exchange books and prepare for the week ahead.
- As a teacher, you may choose to either model the independent reading process, or more likely, use this time to conference individually with readers or meet with small groups.

MATERIALS YOU WILL NEED

- Readily available literature and reading materials

57   Guided Reading

Guided reading places a small group of students of a similar developmental level together for instruction. The ultimate goal in guided reading is to teach the students to use reading strategies independently.

Group four to six readers who are alike enough in their reading development that they can be taught together. Grouping is flexible; students will move in and out as their needs change. Students will read the same teacher-selected text. Note: In choosing the text for guided reading, ensure that it is at the students' *instructional* level: students read with less than 95 percent accuracy. Factors to consider when choosing books for guided reading groups include language and literacy features, sentence complexity, vocabulary, difficulty of words, illustrations, and book and print features.

During guided reading, students receive explicit comprehension-strategy instruction. Strategies might include solving words using graphophonic cues, metacognitive monitoring and correcting, searching for and using information, generating questions, summarizing, predicting, inferring, and critiquing.

Routman (2003) thinks of guided reading as the bridge between shared and independent reading. Determining a student's developmental stage in reading and grouping and instructing according is the key for success. The students are responsible for the reading. The teacher is the guide, observer, monitor, responder, and questioner.

MATERIALS YOU WILL NEED

- Multiple copies of leveled text of any kind
- Dry erase boards, magnetic letters, pens for strategy practice and word work

Writing Centers

Reading/Writing Connection

BACKGROUND

In addition to the goal that children become lifelong readers, they also should become lifelong writers capable of using written language for various purposes. Writing workshops are prevalent in learner-centered classrooms, where students are engaged in different phases of the writing process at varying times. Gone are the days when teachers assign a writing topic and several days later students turn in their papers and receive them back weeks later with red marks and a grade. Instead, with a process approach to writing, teachers model how writers write (how we get ideas; how we plan our writing; how we draft, revise, and edit) and support the novice writers in the classrooms with mini-lessons, response groups, and opportunities to publish some of their writing.

Students can be taught to read like a writer so that pieces of quality children's literature become additional models for writing. Familiarity with different forms of writing supports students' ability to make predictions and read with fluency. Reciprocal skills between reading and writing include understanding purpose, recognizing audience, and knowing the conventions of language. Uninterrupted reading and writing are essential elements in a process-oriented, learner-centered classroom.

58   Readers' and Writers' Workshops

When we think of a workshop, our minds may race to the North Pole, where we imagine busy little elves diligently working at varying stages of toy construction, decoration, packaging, and so on. Few would picture all the elves doing the same thing or total silence as each elf contributes to the production. Similarly, a learner-centered workshop is a buzzing hum of activity, complete with engaged workers doing related yet often unique tasks.

A workshop approach to a period of instructional time looks vastly different from a traditional classroom approach. Structuring a reading workshop or a writing workshop (or a combination of the two) has several key components.

- Whole-group meeting time: Workshop time begins with a *whole-group meeting*, where the teacher sets the stage for the workshop period. The learners' attention is brought to a focus that connects to something done in a previous lesson. During whole-group time, the teacher conducts a ten to fifteen minute mini-lesson on some relevant topic in reading or writing. Students may have an opportunity for guided practice in the large group setting, perhaps with a partner. There may be limited discussion, but generally whole-group time finds the teacher demonstrating a reading or writing strategy or technique that she or he feels is most critical to the students' literacy growth.
- Status of the class: Following the whole group meeting, many teachers take a *status of the class*, quickly calling students' names to hear what that each will be working on. The status of the class provides a level of accountability for the students; they are verbally committing to move forward in their work during this period. A teacher can watch and monitor over several days to ensure that students are, indeed, making progress.
- Reading/writing project time: The bulk of the workshop time follows, with *applied reading or writing*. For thirty to sixty minutes, students work on their individual projects. When appropriate, they are expected to apply

the strategy demonstrated in the mini-lesson. The teacher moves around the room during this time, conferencing with individuals or meeting with small groups. Some teachers choose to conduct guided reading groups during this time as well.

- Whole-group gathering: After the individual project period, workshop time closes with another *whole-group gathering*. Students share *brief oral reports* on their accomplishments or struggles from the day. This sharing exercises speaking and listening skills, builds community, and serves as an informal assessment in determining future workshop directions.

59   Purposeful Tasks

Demonstrate that writing is an important method for communication by engaging students in authentic, purposeful writing tasks. Have students write notes to their parents; letters to fellow students, teachers, or the principal; invitations to a social event; journal entries; or reactions to music or a video. By providing a wide variety of relevant writing experiences, students learn that different purposes require different styles and formats.

Relevant opportunities for writing are plentiful in the learner-centered classroom. Have students do the following:

- Write social letters to their favorite author, a character in a book, a senior citizen, or an international pen pal
- Write persuasive letters in support of a politically or socially appropriate cause
- Write business letters for information on a project they are researching
- Write in personal journals or diaries for self-expression; these might include

   Diaries in which students react to changes inside and around them.

Response journals where they note reactions to content-area information such as a current event, lab experiment, or math problem.

Curiosity journals in which they keep a list of questions of things they would like to know more about.

Literature logs in which they react, with increasing sophistication, to various elements of literature such as characters, plot, and setting.

- Write books for publication in a class or school publishing center

MATERIALS YOU WILL NEED

- Writing materials

60   Published and Unpublished Work

Not all written work becomes a published piece. When students have some choice and flexibility regarding which work to publish and in what format, they display greater perseverance and attention during the editing process. Reviewing students' writing is an important way for you, and for them, to track their progress and establish learning goals. Place samples of students' work in their writing folders and keep them in the writing station for easy access. Students will then choose a piece to publish and work to create a product worth sharing. Students should understand that not choosing to continue with a piece of writing does not constitute failure. Even though you may have a minimum number of published pieces from each student, it is important for them to have some choice in deciding what to publish and how.

Have students experiment with a number of writing formats and keep them in a writing folder. These folders can be filed in a milk crate, cardboard box, or in cereal boxes cut open on the top and two-thirds down one side for ease of storage. Allow students to illustrate their folders to personalize them for easy identification.

Staple student editing checklists and writing guidelines to the writing folders or place them at the writing station. Students should have an opportunity to review and evaluate their work by themselves or with a peer before their writing conferences.

Materials You Will Need

- Folders
- Drawing materials
- Milk crates, cereal boxes, or cardboard boxes
- Editing checklists and writing guidelines

61 Paths to Publication

Finalizing written work for "publication" helps students perceive themselves as writers. Providing different avenues for publishing allows children to see their efforts valued and encourages originality. Students publish their work in a wide variety of formats. They create labels, book jackets, or posters that advertise a favorite book, a class event, or an election campaign. They organize their writing into magazines, book reviews, or research reports to be distributed outside the classroom. Student publications should always be made available to other readers and be added to the variety of class reading resources.

There is a variety of ways to share students' budding writing with others. You may choose to do any of the following:

- Have a special section in the class library for student authors

- Develop a monthly journal, perhaps with rotating themes, that highlights students' work
- Send a class magazine or newspaper home to parents
- Create a riddle book, an etiquette book for students in your grade or school, or an advice column
- Distribute the class reviews of books, music, TV shows, video games, and movies
- Write books to be read to the principal, other adults in the school, or students in other grade levels
- Conduct surveys on student issues, for example,

  "Should students be expected to . . . ?" or

  "How much homework is reasonable?" or

  "My favorite _____."

  Students can publish and post the results in the hallway using graphs with captions.

MATERIALS YOU WILL NEED

- Writing materials
- Drawing materials

Building a Community of Learners

Creating a community of learners is the foundation of effective teaching. You may be passionate about the subject you teach, plan relevant and interesting activities, and deliver fascinating information—but none of this matters if students are afraid to speak up in class, feel that they can't contribute, and don't get the support and encouragement they need to learn.

—National Science Foundation

BACKGROUND

Years ago, when I was nursing my daughter, I had a great deal of time to catch up on reading I had never gotten to. I reread classics and relished contemporary novels, reading new works of familiar authors and discovering new authors who would become lifelong favorites. One of these, John Irving, had just written *The World According to Garp*. After reading it, I recommended it to a good friend with whom I discussed the unfolding story as she progressed through it. I was up with the baby at 2:00 AM one morning when I heard the phone ring. It was my friend, who felt compelled to call and share her shock over a particular—and emotionally moving—passage. Only love of baby and literature could keep me up at that hour! —L. L.

If students are to become lifelong lovers of literature, they need to have an opportunity to discuss what they are reading; to argue, recommend, commiserate, and identify with the characters and their exploits. Students must read a variety of genres and have time to choose their own reading materials. They must also have time to actually read the materials and give and receive feedback on them.

Sharing experiences about reading is vital in developing an appreciation for literature. For young children, literacy development depends on the literacy experiences available to them at home. When schools cultivate partnerships with parents and reach out to the community as a resource, everyone benefits.

Calkins (2001) reminds us that reading is a social activity. The books that matter in our lives are the ones we have discussed with someone else. If we pause and think about the book we are currently reading, we can often find a social connection: Either the book was recommended to us by someone we respect, we can't wait to talk with someone about our views on the book, or we have already had such conversations. Students, too, benefit from opportunities to talk with others about what they are reading. These conversations exercise listening and speaking, enrich clarity of thinking, enhance understanding of the text, and build appreciation for multiple perspectives. They also provide motivation to read some more.

62 Literature Clubs

Literature Clubs is an instructional strategy designed to give learners control over their own reading. Students select books to read and discuss with their peers based on interest rather than reading ability. The teacher acts as a facilitator, at times listening to the student's daily group discussions about their reading. After reading a book, the clubs may design a creative way to share their reading with other classmates, thereby motivating others to choose the book at another time. Students as young as seven years old are able to maintain literature clubs, carrying on meaningful dialogues about books and honoring group-imposed timelines.

Gather four to six copies of several intriguing titles. Briefly discuss each book, perhaps even reading aloud the first chapter so students can sense the flavor of the book. Allow students to indicate first and second choices and then form heterogeneous groups of four to six students. Depending on the length of the titles selected—and age of the students—set a reasonable timeline for completion of the book. Encourage the clubs to break up their texts into readable chunks such as two chapters per day or night. Each day in class, give students time to read and meet with each other to discuss that day's reading. Act as a facilitator, rotating from group to group during their discussions. Be careful not to control or direct the groups; simply listen to their reactions and, if appropriate, offer your feelings about the reading. When the clubs have completed their books, have them develop a creative way to share their reading with the rest of the class. They may perform a commercial for the book, act out a favorite scene, or write a description.

VARIATION

Organize literature clubs so that all groups read related but different titles. For example, students might read different books by the same author or books of the same genre. In this way, a comparative aspect adds dimension to your instruction.

MATERIALS YOU WILL NEED

- Four to six copies each of various books

63   Join the Chorus

Choral reading is a form of shared reading that effectively builds classroom community. Typically found only in the primary grades, choral reading is a powerful motivator for students of all ages and reading abilities. Choral reading is an excellent morning routine, a daily habit that can start students off on a wonderful day. It is a very supportive instructional strategy, promoting the participation of all children, including special education students and second-language learners. The teacher models the reading while students follow the text, allowing students to hear the rhythm and the overall sound of the reading.

Quality poetry is a good choice and will add to the success of choral reading. Collect poems that appeal to your students and transfer them to a transparency or sheet of chart paper or smartboard. Use one poem for several sessions. Introduce the poem by reading it aloud to the class. Reread the poem, inviting students to join in. You may choose to have the students echo you or simply read with you. Read and reread the poem many times, giving out lines to clusters of children, alternating boys and girls, or reading loudly then softly. As students experience repeated readings—which can occur over several days—many of them will memorize the poem. This allows them to focus even more on their oral intonation and presentation.

Once students have had success with the class choral reading, give groups of students another poem. Assign each group the task of preparing a choral performance for the class. Encourage the students to creatively use their voices to reveal the full meaning of the poem. Most students love this routine, and choral reading can quickly develop into a meaningful class ritual, resulting in an increased sense of community in the classroom.

MATERIALS YOU WILL NEED

- Poems
- Transparencies, large chart paper, or smartboard
- Overhead projector
- Felt-tip markers or transparency pens

64   Mine, Yours, and Ours

Developed by Harste, Short, and Burke (1988), this strategy helps students gain understanding of various points of views. It capitalizes on the constructivist concept that asserts that everything we learn is connected to previous learning. Therefore, our understandings and perspectives on things are very personal. Our understandings of the world are influenced by and influence others' understandings of the world. Students need practice defining their own perspectives, recognizing other perspectives, and identifying tensions between the two. Students who appreciate multiple perspectives find the greatest success living in a diverse society.

After students participate in a common experience such as a field trip or reading the same book, have them write a summary of the most significant aspects of that experience. Then, have students work in pairs to compare their summaries and discover connections between them. Encourage students to discuss where they agree and disagree, and what information or interpretations are in one person's summary but not in the other's.

After their discussion, the students can individually or collaboratively write a paragraph explaining the differences they found and why they responded the way they did.

To extend this activity, students can read another book and summarize it the way they think their partner would; read books that present the same story from different perspectives; or take a piece of their own writing and retell the story from someone else's viewpoint.

MATERIALS YOU WILL NEED

- Writing materials

65   Writing Autobiographies

Especially effective early in the school year, having children write and share autobiographies of some kind contributes to building classroom community. As students research their families, consider what is important about them as a classmate, and reflect upon which activities in their lives are most important, the gain a better understanding of themselves and each other. Autobiographies can take a variety of inventive forms, going well beyond the classic essay assignment, "How I Spent My Summer Vacation."

- Creating a life map: A life map is one form of autobiography. On large sheets of paper, students draw small symbols along a timeline representing important events in their lives, from birth to the present. The teacher models the process by creating his or her own life map, describing decisions about what will be included and why. This strategy works with all age groups and is effective for special education and second-language learners because it is all drawing and requires no writing.

- Autobiography of reading: Another option is a reading autobiography, in which students consider their life as a reader, from their earliest recollections to the present. Students can list the earliest books they remember being read to by parents and include significant read alouds from previous teachers. Older students often depict books that have had a deep influence on their lives in some way; many include selections from favorite authors over the past several years.

By sharing their autobiographies with classmates, students are securing a place within the community, enabling others to better understand who they are and why they may act or believe as they do. As an extension, students can be encouraged to write or ask questions for one another, based on the autobiographies

VARIATION

Biography interviews: In this case, students interview another and write biographies rather than autobiographies. They need to learn enough about at least one other student to be able to successfully compose a biography. You might provide structured interview protocols, or let the students develop their own.

MATERIALS YOU WILL NEED

- Pens, pencils, markers
- Large paper

SECTION 5

Assessing Student Growth

Authentic assessment is a continuous operation that is at the heart of teaching and learning. We assess 24/7 and use authentic assessments, such as evidence of kids' work and thinking to guide our teaching and move kids forward.

—Stephanie Harvey and Anne Goudvis

We teach in an unprecedented time of high-stakes testing and school accountability. Never before in the history of American education has the federal government set so much money aside for prescribed programming, and held schools responsible for meeting externally imposed standards of achievement. Test preparation is at an all-time high, as students of all ages spend great portions of their school year practicing for upcoming standardized tests. Far too often, this time spent in test preparation is at the expense of time spent actually reading and writing, which, ironically, is what would most help the students perform well on the test.

Langer (2002) has studied *thoughtful classrooms,* in which students score well on high-stakes assessments though their daily classroom work is interactive and conceptual as opposed to packaged and scripted. Her conclusions suggest that students' engagement in thoughtful reading, writing, and discussion, and their use of knowledge and skills in new situations equates with increased performance, regardless of the school's characteristics or demographics. Not surprisingly, kids who think well test well.

Children engaged in authentic literacy tasks on a regular basis, who continually receive feedback and *just right* instruction, will perform to external standards. Learner-centered teachers depend most heavily on authentic assessment practices but realize that students need some practice and experience with standardized types of assessment if they are to perform well when the state or nation calls. Four to six weeks before an upcoming standardized test, effective teachers begin to introduce testing as a genre to the students. Just as nonfiction text or poetry or historical fiction each presents its own challenges to the reader, so does a standardized test. The pattern of instruction remains the same as it has throughout the year in the literacy workshop. The teacher introduces the new genre (test-taking material); models with think alouds how to navigate this kinds of text; delineates critical attributes of this type of writing; supports the novices as they practice in the new genre; provides many different samples and varieties within the genre; and ultimately develops readers who function independently in the new genre. With this approach to standardized testing, the students do not lose instructional time; they learn transferable skills and strategies to any new type of imposed reading and writing they will meet in their future.

The purpose of any assessment in a learner-centered classroom is to inform instruction. The most effective literacy assessment occurs daily, within the context of real literacy activities, with students exhibiting what they know and don't know about how print works. Instructional decisions are based on children's strengths, weaknesses, and needs. Just as physicians recognize patterns of physical growth in children, learner-centered teachers understand patterns of literacy growth. Neither physician nor teacher is surprised at individual differences among children, yet both are aware of developmental guideposts and can recognize where a child is placed on the developmental continuum. Effective teachers identify students' developmental levels and then structure classroom activities so the students are supported and stretched toward the next level of growth and understanding. Teachers carefully collect and analyze data about students' processes and products in a way that establishes a strong connection between the assessment data and the teacher's instructional plans. Effective teachers realize that growth is not always linear; students will have spurts of growth with peaks and valleys. Information is gathered over time, resulting in a profile of student achievement. Furthermore, effective teachers understand that students' assessment results are a reflection not only of student performance but also of teacher instruction.

Kid-Watching
in the Classroom

BACKGROUND

The most fundamental part of assessment involves careful, systematic observation of students in a variety of contexts. Only through such observation are teachers truly aware of students' growth and progress through the stages of literacy development. Observation should occur in the natural setting of the learning environment and should involve watching, listening, and interacting with students. Teachers notice and record behaviors that students exhibit and later reflect on their observations. Everything a child says and does is a source of information about that child's development.

In recording your observations, use descriptive sentences or phrases. Examples include

- 3/24/07: Patrick is using his pointer finger to track the print in *No, David*.
- 3/24/07: Joanne's narrative piece about Thanksgiving includes characters, setting, and four action events.
- 3/24/07: Josh continues to choose nonfiction in the Reading Center; he's especially into space exploration right now.

Writing objectively and descriptively is the key. Analysis of what you've seen should be done later. When reflecting on these records, you might conclude that Patrick is moving through the emergent stage of reading and may be ready to locate individual words on the page. Your information about Joanne suggests that she has a sense of story and may be ready to experiment with another genre. Josh's behavior reveals that he has found a special interest; depending upon the length of his interest in nonfiction, you may choose to either help him locate more books on this topic or help him find some fiction pieces he might enjoy. Used in such a way, anecdotal records based on *kid-watching* become an important source of planning for the teacher. One advantage of observation is that it is not an obtrusive assessment; it takes place during typical reading and writing events. Knowledge and skills are not the only important points to observe in children; noting their attitudes is equally important.

66   Anecdotal Records

Anecdotal records are brief notes that record observations of actual verbal and nonverbal behaviors. They are descriptive in nature, capturing events with enough detail so the teacher makes evaluations and judgments at a later point. Teachers vary considerably in record content, but most learn to note behaviors that indicate literacy growth (e.g., holding a book right-side-up for the first time, using one's finger as a pointer when reading, using temporary spelling instead of asking the teacher). Useful anecdotal records always involve at least two critical elements: the date and a descriptive comment specific to what the child is doing. Analyzed over time, anecdotal records help the teacher see patterns of growth and development, and allow insight into the child's interests, strengths, and weaknesses.

To take anecdotal records, you must manage the classroom in such a way that students are self-directed and operate without direct instruction or supervision during part of the day. For instance, set up a writers' or readers' workshop or allow students to cycle through various learning stations. This allows you to closely observe a few students a day. Instead of trying to watch everyone doing everything, identify four or five *focus students*. Notice the behaviors and attitudes of these particular students throughout the day. By day's end, you will have rich notes about these few students rather than sparse notes about many. In one week, you should be able to obtain valuable information about each member of your class. When combined with professional teacher judgment, anecdotal records are a valid source of assessment.

MATERIALS YOU WILL NEED

- Record-keeping sheets for each student

67   A Nifty Notebook

There are many ways to manage anecdotal records, but organization is key to the success of this assessment approach. Although individual records do reveal something about the child on a given day, the real power of anecdotal records comes in analyzing the child over a longer period. A collection of six weeks' worth of records offers important information regarding a student's literacy development and indicates what the student needs to move to the next level. Many teachers periodically move notes from an observation notebook into a set of file folders for yearlong storage.

To organize your notes, keep a three-ring notebook with a divider for each student. File the dividers in alphabetical order by the students' last names. Carry this binder with you during conferences. When you meet with a child, turn to his or her section of your notebook and record your information on the pages there. You may wish to write on blank notebook paper or design a page with space designated for comments about reading, writing, attitudes, and other skills and behaviors. Share your observations—both current and past—with the student from time to time, as well as with his or her parents at conferences. Keep your binder very flexible so you can always add more pages as you fill up space or receive new students in your class. If the book becomes too cumbersome, remove some pages and store them in file folders.

MATERIALS YOU WILL NEED

- Three-ring notebook with dividers for each student
- Predesigned record-keeping sheets

68   Sticky Helpers

Developing a workable system of taking and storing anecdotal records is important. Rather than carry around an entire binder full of notebook paper, many teachers have created shortcuts and adaptations. Experiment with different methods so you can find the one most suitable to your needs. You can best capture important information regarding student development by using a variety of collection strategies. A portable system of pages and sticky labels might be one to consider.

Using a clipboard, carry a sheet of mailing labels or a page full of sticky notes. Mailing labels and computer labels are available at warehouse prices when bought in large quantities through office supply catalogs.

As you observe students, write on the labels noting the date, child's name, and your observations. At the end of the day, peel off the labels and place each one on an individual sheet or folder for each student. By writing students' names on the labels at the beginning of a two-week period and peeling the completed ones off at the end of each day, it becomes easy to see who you have yet to observe.

MATERIALS YOU WILL NEED

- Clipboard
- Sheets of mailing labels, computer labels, or sticky notes
- Folders

69   Individual Student Checklists

Checklists make a useful tool for recording observations during or after instruction. They can help inform administrators, parents, and community members about what kinds of behaviors are valued. Some teachers with a depth of understanding about reading and writing create their own checklists. A checklist can indicate to teachers what they should be looking for as signs of literacy growth.

Be aware that a single checklist never includes all the significant behaviors students exhibit. Likewise, many students function successfully without mastering every item on the checklist. Use checklists as a guide, always to be supplemented by anecdotal records.

After deciding which important literacy skills, social skills, and behaviors you wish to see in your classroom, create a checklist. List the behaviors on the left side of a page and title columns across the top as "Not Yet"; "Seldom"; "Sometimes"; "Usually"; and "Always." Having one sheet for each child, review each behavior and mark the individual student accordingly. The result is a "snapshot" of each child on any given day. This checklist makes an effective reference point during individual student and parent conferences, when you focus on the child's strengths and areas for development.

Use checklists early in the semester and at regular intervals to determine student growth.

Materials You Will Need

- Observation checklists for each student

Example:

John Brown	Not Yet	Seldom	Sometimes	Usually	Always
Uses visual information to predict and confirm				X	
Checks illustrations with print					X
Solves unfamiliar words independently		X			
Matches print one to one					X

70 Class Checklists

To get a sense of where your entire class is on specific behaviors and skills, use a class checklist. It provides a picture of students' developing skills and informs your flexible grouping for specific instruction. Information gleaned from a class checklist should always be considered within the context of all of the other assessments taking place in your classroom. The checklist is simply a guide. Differences among students on a class checklist are common; learning occurs in varying stages for everyone.

To create a class checklist, list skills on one side of a sheet of paper and each student's name across the top. As you observe students in your classroom demonstrating specific behaviors, either check off the corresponding box or write in the date of your observation. This way, you will be aware of who has acquired which skills and who may be in need of further instruction. Be aware that checking off a behavior does not mean the student never needs another experience in a certain arena; it simply means that achievement or understanding was demonstrated.

MATERIALS YOU WILL NEED

- Class checklists for various behaviors

Example:

	Joe	Sally	Carlos	Julie	Scott
Uses visual information to predict and confirm	10/2/07	10/2/07	9/2/07		9/14/07
Checks illustrations with print	9/25/07	9/28/07	9/10/07	10/11/07	9/8/07
Solves unfamiliar words independently			10/12/07		
Matches print one to one		9/20/07	yes		9/29/07

71   Historical Checklists

Historical checklists provide a longitudinal look as a student's growth is charted over time. The same checklist provides space for noting a teacher's observations throughout the semester or year. These checklists may be stored in a notebook or inside the cover of each student's portfolio or record folder. Add information at specific times throughout the year as you make student observations. Historical, or longitudinal, checklists make effective reference points for parent conferences. Parents often appreciate the perspective this type of checklist provides as they hear about their child's developing abilities.

To create a historical checklist, list desired behaviors on the left side of a sheet of paper. Across the top, list checkpoint dates, or leave each column blank, to be dated as you make your observations. It is also useful to leave room for qualitative comments on the side or bottom of the page. Mark your calendar at the beginning of the year with the various checkpoints, for example, once a month, to schedule updates of your checklists. You might divide the class into four groups and observe students in each group during a specific week each month. For example, students whose last name begins with A–E would be observed during the first week of the month, and so on.

At the appropriate time, revisit the checklist and consider the student's current overall behavior. Make a comment or note about each specific behavior on the list. Put the checklist aside. Then when the next checkpoint time comes around— usually about one month later—make comments in the next column.

Carefully reflect on each student's growth or lack of growth. Use this information to plan instruction and instructional grouping.

Materials You Will Need

- Student checklists

72   Interviews

Interviews reveal students' thinking about reading and writing. With purposeful probing, a teacher often discovers students' ideas and misconceptions about literacy. Although some students may not be initially aware of what strategies they use when they read or write, interview questions help them become increasingly conscious of their own thinking. With increased teacher modeling of the thought processes underlying reading and writing, the students become increasingly adept at describing their own strategies.

Interviews can be conducted as separate entities or as a natural part of instruction. In a workshop approach to instruction, students are used to having independent conferences with the teacher, so the interview will not be new to them. Oral interviews result in rich information because most students often say more than they write in response to a teacher's questions.

When conducted as a separate entity, an interview consists of a series of prepared questions. One example is Kay Burke's *Reading Inventory* (1994), in which students are asked questions such as these:

- How would you describe yourself as a reader?
- When you are reading and come to something you don't know, what do you do?
- Who do you know who is a good reader? What makes him or her a good reader?
- If you knew someone was having trouble reading, how would you help that person?
- What would your teacher do to help that person?
- How did you learn to read?
- What would you like to do better as a reader?

This interview reveals the students' own view of themselves as readers, as well as their perceptions of the reading process, and it suggests instructional implications. For instance, if a student's responses all focus on sounding out the words, you would know that the child needs a more sophisticated set of reading strategies such as using context clues, skipping a word and coming back, and using illustrations.

Conduct your interviews at the beginning, middle, and end of the year for a developmental view of students' perceptions and growth as readers.

TECHNOLOGY OPTION

Videotape your student interviews. Create a separate tape for each student and conduct a video visit several times during the year.

MATERIALS YOU WILL NEED

- Prepared interview questions
- Video equipment (optional)

73 Open-Ended Questions

When interviews are used as a natural part of instruction, they can be informal and personalized. Interviews commonly occur during conferencing within a readers' or writers' workshop. Orally conducted interviews with individual students allow teachers to probe for specifics and gain an understanding of the student's thinking. Anecdotal records can be kept to document the student's responses. Effective interview questions are nondirective and reflective, probing students' thinking and allowing the teacher to follow their thought processes. There is a wealth of professional literature available about the importance of nonverbal communication. Be aware of what your body language is saying while you question your students; you can be sure they will!

Circulate around your classroom, stopping to visit with individual students. Use open-ended questions such as, tell me what you are doing here or how did you make the decision to use this word? What strategies are you using to solve this problem? As you phrase your questions, remember to avoid the possibility of yes or no answers or to sound as if you are second-guessing the student's response. Ask for clarification and probe, but do not lead, a student. The purpose is to determine what the student thinks, not what you think. Jot down a few notes either during or after the interview so you can reflect on what the student has shared.

When students have the opportunity to share their thinking, they feel a sense of inclusion and importance in your classroom. The added bonus is that, like all quality assessment devices, open-ended questions help you plan your instruction.

Materials You Will Need

- Prepared open-ended questions
- Observation notebook

Student Portfolios

A portfolio is more than just a container full of stuff. It's a systematic and organized collection of evidence used by the teacher and student to monitor growth of the student's knowledge, skills, and attitudes in a specific subject area.

—Linda Vavrus

BACKGROUND

Portfolios are used to assess a student's work over time. Rather than the snapshot you get from a summative test, the portfolio is more like a videotape, providing a holistic view from multiple perspectives. There are several approaches to portfolio assessment, but all entail at least three vital components: collection, selection, and reflection.

Collection refers to the actual gathering of student work throughout the school year. Representations of both process and product are included so the portfolio contains a full range of a student's abilities.

Because it would be impossible to save everything that a student completes during the year, selection is the second critical ingredient. Teachers and students devise criteria to assist them in selecting which materials should be included in the student portfolio. Such selection criteria are vital to the portfolio process; otherwise, the portfolio becomes an overwhelming heap of papers.

Reflection on the portfolio contents, by and with the students, enriches the process and increases the value of this assessment tool.

The power of portfolio assessment lies in the patterns and trends uncovered when analyzing the contents at various points in the year. Growth and expansion of student interests, attitudes, strengths, and weaknesses can be determined and documented through portfolio assessment.

Portfolios are most successful when they are learner centered. Students' active involvement in portfolio assessment increases its value. Students can generate criteria for inclusion and determine the number and type of items to be included. There is potential for parents to be involved by documenting their child's literacy activities at home.

Many teachers keep their own portfolios as a powerful model for students. Teachers' portfolios might contain evidence of their own growth as readers, writers, and professional educators.

74   Crate 'Em Up

Developing a usable system of organizing and maintaining student portfolios is one of the first steps in implementing this type of assessment. Obviously, an effective management system does not ensure quality portfolio assessment, but without such a system, it is very hard to successfully use portfolios. Students should have some ownership in the physical format of their portfolios. Most teachers allow children to decorate their portfolios with markers, crayons, pictures, and photographs.

Organize a system for storing portfolios and their contents. This system can be as simple as having a manila file folder for each student, which can be stored in alphabetical order in a plastic crate of hanging files. If you want a lid, use a cardboard banker's box instead of a plastic crate. A file cabinet also serves this purpose; however, it must be made very clear to the students that they are allowed into this cabinet because they are often not allowed to touch the teacher's file drawers!

Additional options include vertical magazine racks—the type you find in a doctor's waiting room—or an over the door hanging basket system. You might divide the class portfolio and have several in each pocket or basket, with beginning and ending student's name on the outside. This system has the additional advantage of reinforcing alphabetizing skills.

MATERIALS YOU WILL NEED

- Manila file folders for each student
- Hanging files
- Plastic crate or cardboard banker's box
- Other vehicles for hanging storage (optional)

75 Bulky Bundles

In some classrooms, portfolio contents cannot be stored in a flat file folder within a plastic crate. This is the case when students are producing and saving items such as art projects, videotapes, and models of various dimensions. For bulkier portfolios, alternative storage ideas are suggested.

Artist's portfolios, which come in various sizes, are expandable and have flaps that close over the top and tie down. Cardboard tubs—such as large empty ice cream containers—are good to use if your students have many three-dimensional artifacts for their portfolios, such as models and art projects. Many businesses will give teachers cardboard storage boxes and cartons that can be used for portfolios.

For young students who typically include paintings in their portfolios, large under-the-bed cardboard boxes designed for storing wrapping paper or sweaters work well. Teachers who use these often stack the boxes at the back of the room.

Regardless of the storage system used, be sure to have the students decorate their portfolios. Also, allow them access to their contents at all times!

MATERIALS YOU WILL NEED

- Artist's portfolios, cardboard tubs, or large cardboard under-the-bed boxes for each student
- Drawing materials

76 Portfolio Contents

Portfolio assessment begins with key questions teachers must ask of themselves and their students. Such questions drive the entire process of portfolio assessment, setting the parameters for the portfolio. Two key questions determine contents and purpose: What kinds of things should we save for the portfolio? What should we do with all of this stuff?

The portfolio should contain evidence of both student process and student product. Either by grade level or as an entire school, sit down with your colleagues and decide upon some standard pieces that will be placed in every child's portfolio each year. Choose at least three to five items representing process and three to five items representing product. The portfolio contents should reflect the whole student.

Examples of student process include tapes of oral readings, self-assessment sheets, photographs and videos of students in action, drafts that show revision, interview notes, and checklists.

Product measures include logs of books read, written retellings, learning log entries, story maps, photographs of products, graphic organizers, videos of student plays, writing samples, lists of published work, interest inventories, and multimedia presentations the student has created.

Every item in the student's portfolio should demonstrate something about that student's development. If you cannot see something different about the student while comparing one piece to another, remove one. Note: It is important to allow the students choice in selecting some of the pieces to remain in their portfolios.

MATERIALS YOU WILL NEED

- Portfolio folders for each student

77   Portfolio-Prompted Planning

Portfolios connect separate pieces of student work, thereby offering a more complete view of the students themselves. You become aware of students' strengths, and areas for growth can be determined by analyzing the contents of their portfolios. As with any worthwhile assessment venture, the results should point you in the direction of further instructional planning for individual students, flexible groups, and the whole class.

As you become experienced with portfolio assessment, a new way of looking at student work emerges. You see things not for what they are, but for what they reveal about a student's development and what they indicate in terms of needed instruction. As you look at each item, ask yourself, what does this show me that the student knows? What does this show me that the student does not know yet? What do I need to do about that?

For example, an accurately completed story map reflects an understanding of story elements—characters, setting, plot, climax, problem, and solution. If several students' maps show misunderstanding of plot, a mini-lesson with that group of children is in order.

A revised writing sample might show a student's understanding of how to use description as an elaboration strategy. If you see that a student continuously uses only description for elaboration, further instruction about comparison, hyperbole, exaggeration, and action verbs may be necessary. If, on the other hand, you see that the student uses different types of elaboration in several writing samples, perhaps the student could teach a small group of less successful writers how to use these strategies.

A list of books read in the last semester reveals a student's propensity toward a particular genre and the quantity of a student's reading. You may wish to intervene by suggesting other genres or by setting some minimum requirements for the number of books read in the upcoming weeks.

Analysis of portfolio contents combines powerfully with effective instructional planning.

MATERIALS YOU WILL NEED

- Student portfolios

78   Entry Slips

When students have a voice in their classroom, they gradually assume more and more responsibility for their own learning. There should be a careful balance between items the students choose for their portfolios and items the teacher chooses.

Allowing children to choose items for their portfolios personalizes the collection and builds confidence in their decision-making skills. You are also demonstrating confidence that they will choose items that reflect special things about them as individuals. Portfolio entry slips offer important insight into what the children value and believe you value about their learning. All of these aspects are important as you instruct and evaluate your students.

Structure periodic sessions for students to work on their portfolios. Tell the students that they will choose an item for their portfolio from their week's work. Guide them through a review of what has been accomplished. Encourage them to look through their desks and daily folders to remind themselves of what they have done. Stress that portfolio items do not have to be finished pieces of work; rather, they are things that tell something about themselves as learners.

Using either large sticky notes or half-sheets of paper that can be stapled to the item, have students write a portfolio entry slip. On this slip of paper, instruct students to briefly describe why each item has been chosen for the portfolio. After everyone has completed an entry slip, invite several students to share their comments with the group. Student share-outs provide an opportunity for you to validate appropriately written slips and model how to write improved ones. The process of writing portfolio entry slips provides students with practice in one of our ultimate goals: self-evaluation!

VARIATION

Use a structured, inquiry-driven entry slip. For example, include questions such as, what does this item show about me as a learner? How did I go about creating this item? How is this item different from my other work? What did I learn from working on this item?

MATERIALS YOU WILL NEED

- Large sticky notes or half-sheets of paper
- Pencils
- Stapler

79   Autobiographies of Work

Throughout the school year, have students review their entire portfolios and draw conclusions about their learning and improvement. This allows students to see the big picture and notice areas of growth that may not be visible on a day-to-day basis. Students step out of the role of portfolio creator and become an analyzer. After reviewing all of the portfolio contents, students write an autobiography of the work inside, describing how it has changed over time. This helps students develop an evaluative voice and increases their responsibility for their own learning and growth.

Students as young as kindergartners can look at several pieces of work over time and make some conclusive statements about their growth and learning.

At least once each semester, students should review their entire portfolios and create a written evaluation. For younger students, effective methods for self-evaluation include filling in a structured worksheet or circling an icon, for example, a smiling face, neutral face, or frown.

One way to initiate the autobiographies-of-work process is to have students find a spot in the room to spread out their portfolio contents. After reading each item in the portfolio, have the students organize them into categories (e.g., most successful to least successful) according to their point of view. In reviewing the items, students should consider the following questions:

- Why is this piece better than that one?
- What did I do differently in this piece?
- What is most striking about this piece?
- What can I say about my improvement from my least successful piece to my most successful?
- How have I grown?
- What would I still like to improve upon?

After guiding students through this process of analyzing and reflecting, ask them to write an autobiography of the work inside the portfolio. These autobiographies can be the focal point for parent-teacher conferencing or for student-led conferences in which the students explain their portfolios to their parents at conference time.

MATERIALS YOU WILL NEED

- Student portfolios
- Writing materials

80   Biographies of Work

In most learner-centered classrooms, it doesn't take long for students to see themselves as a community of learners. When students collaborate, the level of learning and relationship is enriched. In this environment, peer assessment techniques can be quite valuable. With appropriate structure and modeling, students are usually very honest and straightforward, learning from and with each other as they conduct peer conferences.

One way to structure peer conferences is to have students create biographies of work. This strategy is an alternative to autobiographies of work (see Strategy 79). Biographies of work require the same type of evaluative process—but this time the reviewer is not the author but rather a trusted peer.

Allow each student to choose a partner he or she trusts and respects. Guide the students through the process and questions in autobiographies of work, substituting "the author" for "you." For example, you would say, "What did the author do differently in this piece?" or "How has the author grown?" Students look through their partner's work, analyze what they see, and jot down notes.

After the series of prompted questions by the teacher, each student then writes a biography of work for the student with which he or she is paired. This strategy could be used once a semester and can be alternated with autobiographies of work.

MATERIALS YOU WILL NEED

- Student portfolios
- Writing materials

Exhibitions and Performance Tasks

By changing the way we look at assessment, we will transform our classrooms into places where we know that students will experience learning to the fullest and acquire the knowledge and skills necessary to be vital, contributing members of society.

—Barbara Talbert Jackson

As world-class academic standards continue to become more and more prominent in our twenty-first century schools, so are many nonacademic competencies viewed as necessary for success in the modern workplace. Skills such as creative thinking, decision making, problem solving, learning how to learn, collaboration, information literacy, and self-management have been defined as necessary by the U.S. Department of Labor. Traditional assessment approaches fall short in their ability to measure such competencies. Teachers need some viable assessment alternatives in which students demonstrate their understanding by doing more than simply choosing the right answer. Performance assessment is one such alternative.

Performance assessment is based on authentic tasks: simulations, exercises, or problems that require students to demonstrate their understanding and apply their skills and knowledge as they would in the world outside of school.

Frequently, these assessments occur over time and result in a tangible product or observable performance. They encourage self-evaluation and revision, require judgment to score, reveal degrees of proficiency based on established criteria, and make the scoring criteria public. Consistent with a learner-centered approach, performance tasks require students to construct new knowledge, allowing for diverse responses based on individual experience.

81   Building In Authenticity

Authenticity is one of the hallmarks of performance assessment. Authentic assessment engages students in applying knowledge and skills in the same way they are used in the real world outside of school. Performance assessment bridges the gap between school and reality, and is designed to prepare students for success in both arenas. For example, rather than having students list the ten ingredients to a collaborative relationship, authentic assessment asks students to work together to solve a real-life problem. The teacher then notes which of the ten ingredients the students utilized. Although most typical classroom tasks require a single thirty- to sixty-minute class period, authentic performance assessment tasks may take several weeks to complete.

The principal can become part of the performance-task process. The message sent to children is: We value what you are doing. Your success is important to the entire leadership of this school.

STRATEGY

To create authentic performance assessment tasks, first identify the standards the assessment will measure. Your content standards, often district, state or province driven, will include both *declarative knowledge* (content information) and *procedural knowledge* (understanding how to do something). For example, a declarative content standard would be the student will understand that the Civil War had many causes. A procedural standard would ask the student to convert measurements in the English system to the metric system.

After determining which standards you are trying to measure, structure the performance task around a complex reasoning processes such as the following:

- Comparing
- Classifying
- Inducing
- Deducing
- Analyzing
- Decision making
- Investigating
- Problem solving
- Constructing support
- Experimenting
- Inventing

Choose the reasoning process that most closely correlates with your identified standard.

The next step is to draft a performance task. Using the Civil War example from above, the task could focus on constructing support. For example, "Refute or support the claim that slavery was the major cause of the Civil War." If you wanted to focus on comparing, you might use this kind of task: "Discuss three of the causes of the Civil War and determine whether they were related."

Next, build in some information-gathering requirements. Performance assessment is most authentic when it demands students to collect and process information from a multiplicity of sources. We constantly want our students to discriminate among various sources of information, so a statement such as the following is often an important part of this type of assessment: "As you review the causes of the Civil War, keep a list of your sources (people, articles, books, tapes, etc.), and make notes as to their worthiness and usefulness to you. Be prepared to share this information orally."

Just as in the real world, where people must weigh the validity of differing opinions and defend their own decisions, students gain practice in this arena as they complete their task.

Finally, decide how students will communicate their performance. Depending on the task itself, students can demonstrate their understandings in a variety of ways. Offer students a choice of several possibilities for presenting their information. Possibilities include the following:

- Written reports
- Letters
- Articles
- Videotapes
- Audiotapes
- Newscasts
- Mock interviews
- Dramatic presentations
- How-to manuals

After writing your final draft of the performance assessment, give it to the students as a natural part of instruction. Along with their assignment, students must have a copy of the criteria you will use to judge their performance. Determine the logistics and scheduling for the students' preparation and presentation. The audience for the presentation may be the whole class; a selected group of students; a team of teachers, including the principal; or any combination of these groups. Evaluating the performance will involve some judgment on the part of the audience—and self-evaluation on the part of the presenter—but should be done with respect to the preestablished set of criteria. Rubrics are important tools for this purpose (see Strategy 83: "Developing a Rubric").

In developing performance assessment tasks, one's approach to curriculum and instruction is naturally shifted. You first must consider the assessment method related to the expected performance and then backwards map to consider what is the most important knowledge to be emphasized and what skills and strategies must be developed so that students can use this knowledge in a meaningful way.

MATERIALS YOU WILL NEED

- Materials dependent on performance tasks offered

82   Anchors and Archetypes

Research on effective lesson design strongly supports the notion of modeling for students. As in all aspects of life, we are much more successful when we know what we are shooting for and how close our attempt is to the target or standard. Anchors and archetypes give students successful examples of what they are expected to accomplish.

One effective way to build your collection of anchors and archetypes is to save copies of outstanding work from your class to be used with next year's students. It is important to periodically compare your anchors with those of other teachers in your grade level to ensure that you are consistent in your expectations for excellence.

Although anchors and archetypes can be used in any subject area, they work especially well when using holistic scoring for writing. A set of anchor papers contains several compositions that illustrate each level of possible scoring. For instance, using a four-point holistic scale, your anchor set should include at least three 1s, three 2s, three 3s and three 4s. Each paper with a 1 should have received it for different reasons and so on for 2s, 3s, and 4s. The assumption is that there is an established set of criteria for each scoring level. Use these anchor papers when introducing a writing assignment to students. As you display a transparency of each anchor paper, lead a discussion regarding its score.

Once you are confident that students understand the criteria, anchor papers can be laminated for students to use as they draft and revise their own work. Remind them to read their papers and then read one of the 4s to make sure their work meets the criteria. Encourage students to score their own papers before turning them in to you.

Use the anchors to score your students' writing. Also use them to encourage your students to think aloud about their work as they become increasingly aware of what they are or are not doing in their writing.

MATERIALS YOU WILL NEED

- Transparencies and photocopies of anchor papers
- Student work

83   Developing a Rubric

As teachers engage in more alternative, authentic assessment measures, a single correct answer becomes less and less predominant. As a result, there is a need for some direction in judging student performance. Students exhibit even a well-defined set of criteria to varying degrees. As in a gymnastics meet, where each person uses the same standard—certain moves for the routine—judges score each performer with respect to a shared set of criteria. Both gymnasts and judges know beforehand what constitutes an outstanding backflip versus a mediocre one. This same concept applies to classroom performance assessment.

A *rubric* is a fixed scale and a list of characteristics that describe performance for each of the points on the scale. The intention of this tool is to increase objectivity in teacher scoring. *Rubric* comes from the Latin term *rubrica terra*, referring to the use of red earth centuries ago to mark or signify something of importance. Because rubrics describe levels of performance, they provide important information to teachers, parents, and all stakeholders interested in knowing what students can do. For the students, rubrics promote learning by offering clear performance targets for agreed-upon standards. The rubric used for assessment should be presented to students along with their assignment.

The number of points on the scale of a rubric can range from three to six. Many experts recommend you use an even number of points so you are not tempted to mark most students in the middle. This way, you force yourself to decide whether the student is above average in performance. If you were to use an odd number of points, for instance five, you might be inclined to mark most of your students as 3s. Usually one level of performance on the rubric is considered acceptable; for example, when using a four-point scale, a 3 or above is often deemed an acceptable performance. The most important factor to keep in mind when creating a rubric is to clearly define and share the criteria for each performance level with students before they even begin their work!

MATERIALS YOU WILL NEED

- Prepared rubrics

Presentation Rubric Sample

Evaluating Student Presentations

	1	2	3	4	Total
Organization	Audience cannot understand presentation because there is no sequence of information.	Audience has difficulty following presentation because student jumps around.	Student presents information in logical sequence that audience can follow.	Student presents information in logical, interesting sequence that audience can follow.	
Subject Knowledge	Student does not have grasp of information; student cannot answer questions about subject.	Student is uncomfortable with information and is able to answer only rudimentary questions.	Student is at ease with expected answers to all questions but fails to elaborate.	Student demonstrates full knowledge (more than required) by answering all class questions with explanations and elaboration.	
Graphics	Student uses superfluous graphics or no graphics.	Student occasionally uses graphics that rarely support text and presentation.	Student's graphics relate to text and presentation.	Student's graphics explain and reinforce screen text and presentation.	
Mechanics	Student's presentation has four or more spelling errors or grammatical errors.	Presentation has three misspellings or grammatical errors.	Presentation has no more than two misspellings or grammatical errors.	Presentation has no misspellings or grammatical errors.	
Eye Contact	Student reads all of report with no eye contact.	Student occasionally uses eye contact but still reads most of report.	Student maintains eye contact most of the time but frequently returns to notes.	Student maintains eye contact with audience, seldom returning to notes.	
Elocution	Student mumbles, incorrectly pronounces terms, and speaks too quietly for students in the back of class to hear.	Student's voice is low. Student incorrectly pronounces terms. Audience members have difficulty hearing presentation.	Student's voice is clear. Student pronounces most words correctly. Most audience members can hear presentation.	Student uses a clear voice and correct, precise pronunciation of terms so that all audience members can hear presentation.	
				Total Points:	

SOURCE: Developed by Information Technology Evaluation Services, NC Department of Public Instruction

Here are Web sites helpful for creating and using rubrics:

http://www.ncsu.edu/midlink/ho.html

http://school.discovery.com/schrockguide/assess.html

http://www.teach-nology.com/web_tools/rubrics/

http://rubrics4teachers.com/

http://www.tcet.unt.edu/START/instruct/general/
rubrics.htm

84   Exciting Exhibitions

Exhibitions are an extension of performance assessments. As
with all performance assessment, application of what has been
learned is required. An exhibition requires students to combine their learning from various disciplines and from life itself
and to demonstrate their understanding to an audience.
Teachers create exhibitions by determining what qualities and
abilities they value in students and by designing the means
with which they can be viewed. When students know what is
expected, and it is cast in an interesting light, the goal becomes
more appealing and attainable. Exhibitions give students
involvement with real and complex issues—much like they
will confront outside of school.

To design an exciting exhibition, first decide what it is you
want to see from your students. Move beyond behavioral
objectives and reflect on the qualities, attributes, and disposi-
tions of successful students. These may include their confidence in presenting to a group, the ability to read and compare
various sources, or a knack for figuring out a math problem in
an original way.

Consider issues pertinent to your students and create challenges for them. In presenting the exhibition assignments, be
prepared to show successful examples, as in anchors and

archetypes (see Strategy 82) and explain the scoring criteria that will be used.

Discuss the timeline with the students and clarify whether students may work together. Your exhibitions may be focused on a particular content, but they should require the integration of conceptual understandings from a variety of content areas.

Exhibition

An exhibition following an ecological unit of study (at any grade level) may include the following:

- A display of cleaned out real trash items mounted on a board
- Labels on each piece indicating recyclability
- Written explanation of why each item is good/bad for the environment
- Statistics related to amount of trash collected in neighborhood/community/city/state/country
- Mathematical projections about continued increases of trash or increase in recycling
- Examples of persuasive letters that could be written to local officials, parents, classmates, state, and national leaders
- Collected articles about communities highly involved in recycling, with benefits highlighted by student
- Photographs of students or classes involved in recycling efforts at home or school

MATERIALS YOU WILL NEED

- Materials dependent on exhibitions planned

Leading Learning-Focused Conversations

Strategies for Professional Development

The ability to start, structure, and sustain thinking in meaningful conversations marks the difference between a well-meaning colleague who dispenses advice and a teacher leader who ignites learning.
—Laura Lipton and Bruce Wellman

L iteracy specialists have a unique opportunity to influence positive change and growth for teachers that results in more confident, successful, literate students. In addition, creating professional communities where examination of data and exploration of instructional strategies is the norm is a powerful and compelling goal.

However, school-based instructional specialists face a variety of challenges in their emerging role as the first line of support for classroom and school improvement efforts. Enthusiasm alone will not suffice; neither will deep technical knowledge. Literacy specialists are often given project responsibility without the authority required to direct instructional changes. They must struggle between the pressure to fix immediate problems while raising achievement scores, and the desire to promote an ongoing spirit of learning within the school community. In many cases, the "teacher down the hall" is suddenly transformed into the expert who visits classrooms and dispenses advice.

As they redefine their relationships with peers, literacy leaders are working to overcome deep norms of privacy that make visits from others unwelcome no matter how well intended. To accomplish this transition requires the relational skills and tools for working successfully with both beginning and experienced colleagues.

Skillful specialists begin learning interactions, whether in one-to-one or group configurations, by focusing attention, clarifying expectations, and activating both emotional and cognitive readiness to engage. Several key approaches are useful to keep in mind as these goals are accomplished.

START WITH *THEIR* STUFF

Begin your conversations or meetings by inquiring about the present literacy levels, student profiles, and instructional approaches of the teachers you work with. Avoid initiating advice, instruction, or suggestions until you have a clear sense of their perspectives and their contexts, individually and collectively.

START WITH SUCCESS

Explore data, share anecdotes, and illuminate practices that reflect positive gains in student achievement. In this way, you build on a foundation of what works. Identify effective choices and strategies, and seek areas for transfer of identified successes to areas of challenge.

PROVIDE CHOICE

Even when a project includes nonnegotiable aspects (e.g., a prescribed schedule will be adhered to, particular instructional strategies will be implemented, specific curricular objectives will be taught), there is still room for choice. Look for flexibility within schedule parameters; have colleagues choose which strategies they'd like to learn first; discuss differentiation and flexible approaches to curricular objectives. Preserve choice, as well, in your relationships. That you will meet may be a given; however, where, when, and how often to meet, for example, can all be optional.

REDUCE SCOPE AND DURATION

Often a new initiative seems daunting. The perception that everything must change all at once can be overwhelming for new and experienced teachers alike. When orchestrating program or instructional changes, suggest starting points that allow teachers to begin but not overhaul everything they are doing, and plan for time frames that allow for reflection and learning. For example, if you are initiating learning centers with the ultimate goal of center-driven instruction, support teachers in choosing one center to start with, and determine a time period, say three weeks, that they would use to determine the effectiveness of the center and explore ways it is working (or not) with their students.

Generally, beginning on a smaller scale helps colleagues move forward, and small successes help keep them moving in that direction.

USE DATA/THIRD POINT TO DEPERSONALIZE AND FOCUS

Student work products, short-cycle assessments, and state and district test results all serve to focus and ground conversations about student progress. Use these data as a third point; that is, place the data in the center of your conversations—whether one to one or full group—and use them as a reference point for analyzing present practice and choosing next steps toward continuous improvement. Using neutral pronouns, such as *these* data or *these* results, rather than *your* data or even *our* results, depersonalizes the conversation and aligns the literacy specialist with the group members in their shared effort to produce student gains.

ASK MORE THAN TELL

Begin and end your learning-focused conversations with questions. These don't have to be widely open ended but can focus on the topic at hand. Start by inquiring about your colleagues' perspectives related to the topic (e.g., shared reading) and end by asking your colleagues to summarize what they're taking away from a session or by determining any resources they might require or by naming their next steps. In this way, conversations and meetings begin and end with them, not you.

Crafting the Container

Starting, Structuring, and Sustaining Thinking

BACKGROUND

The work of literacy specialists can sometimes be perceived as corrective, or remedial. That is, introducing changes in practice suggests that the current practice is somehow inadequate or wrong. Understanding this emotional response can be useful when you approach colleagues with new literacy initiatives, newly adopted programs, or even new instructional ideas.

Attending to the emotional resourcefulness of colleagues is just as important as addressing their classroom practice, perhaps even more important. Listening nonjudgmentally, and with full attention, to colleagues' perspectives on their students and their current approaches to literacy instruction is a sign of respect and often an effective way to open the door to deeper conversation. Focusing these conversations on students, using various sources of data, and calibrating the discussion with specific standards and clear expectations for learners helps to depersonalize the interaction and reduce some of the potential pushback reactions.

The worksheets in this section serve as a tangible third point, providing a visual reference to focus conversations and stimulate thinking while aligning the literacy specialist with the group or group member.

85   Simple Stem Completions

Starting with the experience or perspective of your colleagues is a positive way to assess their attitudes and approaches to literacy. Simple strategies that don't require a lot of preparation are practical and effective. Using worksheets or even index cards provides an external focus for your conversations about practice. One way to accomplish this is by asking teachers to complete sentence stems and bring them to your sessions, whether the meeting is one-to-one or small group. Note that the stems are generic and flexible, and can be adapted to any relevant topic (e.g., guided reading, vocabulary development, oral reading, classroom-based assessment, English-language learners).

The stems can be exchanged in advance of a meeting via e-mail or even completed at the beginning of the session.

Stems might include:

- When I think about this topic, I'm curious about . . .
- Given this topic, I'd like to know more about . . .
- For us as a grade-level team, I'm hoping . . .
- One thing I became aware of this week is . . .
- As I've applied the new reading strategies this week, I've discovered . . .

MATERIALS YOU WILL NEED

- 3" × 5" index cards, Post-it notes, or preprinted stem completion sheets

86   T-Chart Opposites

Using a T-chart worksheet to set up juxtapositions or opposites surfaces perspectives and provides an opportunity to examine them in a psychologically safe way. Use individual worksheets or a chart pad and stand for group work. For example, individuals can complete their own worksheets or generate just one item on each side of their list. Then a master list can be charted. Or, juxtapositions can be brainstormed and recorded directly onto the chart by you or another group member.

The topic should be whatever is timely and relevant to the group, for example, any current literacy initiative or something that teachers are presently trying out in their classrooms. The topic would appear on the top of the chart or worksheet.

Effective opposites include:

- Hopes/Fears
- Strengths/Stretches
- Successes/Challenges
- Pros/Cons

MATERIALS YOU WILL NEED

- Chart pad and felt-tip markers
- Individual T-chart worksheets, if desired

87   3-2-1

3-2-1, originally a classroom-based strategy, transfers effectively to one-to-one or small-group conversations. The structured worksheet provides a stimulus for engaging with experiences, perspectives, reactions—in fact, whatever the topic and discussion might call for.

This strategy also works well when you can't meet face to face but want to engage thoughtfully with colleagues or prepare for a sit-down conversation at some point.

Depending on how you organize the prompts, 3-2-1 is a simple structure for planning, reflecting, or shared problem solving.

For example, for planning, try

3 goals for my students this week
2 strategies I expect to apply
1 methods for assessing student success

For reflecting, try

As a result of applying the new vocabulary strategies,
3 changes I noticed in my struggling students
2 things I'd be sure to try again
1 thing I might change or add

For problem solving, try

3 things that are challenges for my students
2 things that might be causing these issues
1 question/strategy I would like to explore

MATERIALS YOU WILL NEED

- Structured 3-2-1 worksheets

88   Mindful Memorandum

Most literacy specialists serve multiple grade levels or even full staffs. Carving time to address the immediate needs of colleagues—as well as opportunities for thoughtful, in-depth conversations—can be daunting. With its priority gauge, the mindful memorandum is effective in flagging urgent problems. Further, the priority is determined by the requester and requires concise and clear articulation of the topic at hand, which ultimately leads to a more productive, time-efficient interaction.

Mindful memorandums can be supplied to staff members early in the school year, with an explanation of their use, or available near the literacy specialist's mailbox. Alternatively, the mindful memorandum format can be mounted on an e-mail server or as a fill-in pdf file for ease of use.

Mindful Memorandum

To:	From:	Date:

Hottest Topic of the Moment:

Questions/Concerns/Successes

Priority Gauge:
☐ Need To Talk Now!   ☐ When You Can, But Soon   ☐ Whenever

Mentor's Response

To:	From:	Date:

Response/Comments:

SOURCE: Lipton, L., and Wellman, B. (2003). *Mentoring Matters: A Practical Guide to Learning-Focused Relationships*. Sherman, CT: MiraVia, LLC. Copyright © MiraVia, LLC. Used with permission.

89   Brainstorm and Pass

Brainstorming is an efficient way to generate lots of ideas before making choices or narrowing a focus for further exploration of a topic. However, structuring brainstorm sessions for balanced participation can be challenging, especially when there are very experienced, or even very vocal, group members. Brainstorm and pass is an effective strategy for including all voices in generating ideas.

Introduce the strategy and be sure to add your purpose and intention for applying it. That is, you will be brainstorming for a few minutes and you are offering a structure to ensure that all voices can be heard. A bonus rationale is that this strategy also transfers very effectively for successful brainstorming in the classroom.

Initiate the topic to be addressed. Explain that the brainstorming will go in a round-robin fashion, moving to the right. Group members can add an item or say, "Pass." Be sure to caution the group that they should wait for colleagues and not jump in to save them. Someone who has passed is still included in subsequent rounds. Continue the process for several times around the group.

Lists can be question driven, for example,

- What most influences student success in reading (or writing)?
- What are some effective classroom-based assessment tools?
- What are some factors that we might address related to home-school partnerships?
- What are some things that challenge our English-language learners using our present reading protocols?

Other lists can be topic focused:

- Things in our reading instruction we feel confident about at this time
- Questions we have about _____

- Quick and inexpensive bulletin board ideas
- Supplemental reading materials

If you are facilitating a large group, structure groups of four to six participants, and have each group brainstorm its own lists. Then ask each group to choose several ideas it would like to contribute. Record these on a chart pad to use with the full group.

MATERIALS YOU WILL NEED

- Paper, pens
- Chart pad
- Felt-tip markers

90   Problem-Solving Partnerships

Learning-focused relationships are reciprocal. When experience, expertise, and new ideas are generated collaboratively, everyone benefits and everyone learns. Structuring problem solving sessions that tap the existing expertise of experienced professionals, and contributing to those ideas with your own technical support, can be a productive and satisfying way to build relationships, influence practice, and improve student learning. Groups can be grade-level teams, vertical teams, departments, or a gathering of interested volunteers. Groups of approximately six to eight participants will be most efficient and effective.

For problem solving partnerships, organize a meeting time when each participant will bring a presenting challenge or issue to the session. During the meeting, each member briefly shares the problem. The group then discusses and surfaces the desired outcome in specific behavioral terms. For example, a member might describe a student who refuses to work collaboratively.

Next, group members brainstorm options for achieving the outcome. Brainstorming eliminates judgment and reduces certainty, thereby opening up space for lots of ideas.

Finally, discuss criteria, pros and cons, and other points for determining which idea or ideas are most viable.

The problem presenter then determines next steps. This can be done during the meeting or after an opportunity to think about the input.

The process should take approximately fifteen minutes and is then repeated, as time allows, for each participant. Groups of six to eight participants will be most efficient and effective.

91   Going Graphic

Visual organizers such as Venn diagrams or semantic webs are effective ways to center conversations and generate rich exchanges. Worksheets serve to structure engagement and focus thinking. For example, rather than asking colleagues to have a discussion comparing and contrasting their present practice to the new expectations or one group of students with another, have them create a Venn diagram. Organize partners using a worksheet, or small work groups using a chart pad so the information is visually vibrant and accessible to all participants.

Try a Venn diagram for comparing and contrasting:

- Students in different reading groups
- Past practice to present initiatives
- Grade-level curricula
- Various instructional materials or methods
- Present practice to future expectations

MATERIALS YOU WILL NEED

- Graphic organizer worksheets
- Chart pads
- Felt-tip markers

Learning-Focused
Consultation

Literacy specialists are often called upon to share technical expertise, supply information, identify and offer expert analysis of any achievement gaps, and provide solutions to complex problems. How these various functions are approached can influence the degree to which the specialist's ideas are accepted and implemented, and, more important, the degree to which this information produces greater learning for teachers. Telling and advising is less effective than sharing and exploring. Consulting without a focus on learning can build dependency on the literacy specialist for problem solving. Advice without explanation of the underlying choice points and guiding principles usually does not develop teachers' abilities to transfer learning to new settings or, ultimately, to generate their own solutions.

When specialists take a consulting stance, there is still a great deal of room for producing learning beyond the immediate fix. Enduring understandings and a greater capacity for independent problem solving and decision making can also be achieved. Offering choice, thinking aloud about cause-effect relationships, and making clear and specific connections to effective principles of literacy development all contribute to authentic professional development.

Although information and problem solving are useful supports to offer, if overdone, they rob teachers of opportunities to learn from experience. Consultation that is learning-focused offers immediate support as well as tools and approaches for tackling future problems with increasing independence. This approach is as valid for novices as it is for highly experienced practitioners. Clarity of your intention to support learning and growth must be established, and congruent behaviors must be displayed. It is futile to express a desire to produce growth and then proceed to tell teachers what to do.

92   An Idea Menu

When a solution to a problem is requested, a menu of ideas—ideally, at least three—produces choice, flexibility, and conditions for further learning. Suggesting multiple options when planning or problem solving provides information and support while placing the responsibility for the choice of action or alternative with your colleagues.

Discussing the criteria or the pros and cons of a particular choice extends the learning opportunity and embeds those criteria for future choice making.

For example, sharing ideas for classroom-based assessment might sound like this: "There are several possibilities that might work in your classroom; you might use some kid-watching, choosing several students and keep running records on them, or you might develop a writing rubric with the students and have them assess their own work along with you, or possibly keep individual portfolios and jot notes on students as you observe them working. Date the notes and slip them into the portfolios daily, or even weekly."

It is useful at this point to inquire about which choice would be most appealing or most effective in your colleague's classroom and then engage in planning for whichever option is chosen.

93 Make Your Thinking Transparent

The power of thinking out loud is well documented in classroom practice. For example, strategies for reading comprehension are modeled when teachers think out loud about their approach when they come to something they don't know or understand in a text. These think alouds give young learners the benefit of the teacher's expertise and provide them with skills and approaches for their own engagement with text.

This same result is achieved when literacy specialists are confronted with a problem or instructional challenge. By making your thinking transparent, you allow access to your experience and expertise as a lens for colleagues as they consider approaches to instructional planning and problem solving. Sharing your thought process along with a solution or idea provides insights that would otherwise be unavailable to your colleagues. This simple approach provides learning beyond the specific event and maximizes the likelihood of transfer to future applications.

Also consider reflecting out loud. Include things you have learned, mistakes you have made, and how you have corrected or adjusted goals you have set for your own learning, and some reasons why.

94 Patterned Response: What, Why, How

Literacy specialists are frequently called upon to be advisers or problem solvers. Providing solutions, especially when you have technical expertise and great passion for student learning, is very compelling. This drive to fix is often compounded by the apparent and pressing needs observed in classrooms and the desire to reduce the burdens of busy teachers.

When sharing expertise as a learning-focused literacy specialist, an effective verbal pattern includes describing the *what, why, and how* of an idea or solution (Lipton & Wellman, 2003). This might sound like this: "Here is a strategy for addressing that issue (what), which is likely to be effective because (why), and here is one way you might apply it (how)."

For example: "It's important to get attention first before giving verbal directions (what). This is important because eliminating distractions and preparing students to listen increases their focus and readiness to begin a task. This increases both time on task and success for more learners (why). One strategy for getting attention that might be effective with your second graders is a soft clapping countdown. Begin with four loud claps, followed by three a bit softer, and then two claps even softer, and finally one gentle clap for ready. Students join in when the first claps begin and are expected to be focused and ready by the final clap (how)."

95   The Big Idea

When offering a suggestion or solution, be sure to add the principle of literacy practice that relates to the idea. Principles of practice include theoretical constructs, conceptual understandings, and information on student development. As teachers internalize principles of learning and teaching, these overarching lenses become mental resources for independently generating approaches and solutions.

Connecting a specific strategy or solution to the broader principles of effective practice provides an opportunity to learn and apply the principle, as well as the individual idea, in other situations. This might sound like this: "An important principle of practice related to (topic) is _____; so a strategy like (suggestion) should be effective in this situation."

You can combine offering a principle of practice with a menu approach, which increases the invitational quality and learning potential. For example: "An important principle of practice related to formative, classroom-based assessment is that the assessment should be partnered with instruction, not separate from it. So, with your fourth graders, you might use a graphic organizer like a Venn diagram to assess their ability to compare characters in a story; or an observational checklist during guided reading; or a rubric attached to a sample of their writing."

96   Categorically Speaking

Ideas or solutions as categories provide a wider range of choice and a richer opportunity for learning than discrete strategies or applications. For example, a category such as *grouping students* is broader than *putting students in pairs*. Putting students in pairs is even broader than suggesting a specific partnering strategy. When broad categories are offered, there is more opportunity for your colleagues to develop personally relevant applications. Thus working within parameters (e.g., there will be interactive groups), teachers can devise methods that appeal to their own teaching style.

This approach is especially effective when several categories are offered, similar to an idea menu (see Strategy 92). For example, imagine you're working with a first grade teacher talking about self-directed workstations. She can't think of methods for keeping her students independently engaged. Rather than specific activities, you suggest that perhaps something they might cut and paste or put together with puzzle pieces or color in on a worksheet would be effective. The teacher can then choose one of these modes and create a specific activity based on her curricular outcomes at that time.

97   Sharing Causal Theories

Exploring and understanding the root causes of a problem accelerate solving the specific presenting problem and often allow for more effective, proactive planning to avoid similar problems in the future. Thus when a colleague presents a problematic issue, rather than suggesting potential solutions, it can be very productive to offer several factors that might be producing the problem. This option is particularly effective when working with experienced teachers because it respectfully indicates your awareness that they have a rich background to draw upon and invites their engagement as coproblem solvers.

This might sound like this: "There are several things that typically would produce that behavior (or result); for example _____, _____, or _____."

Followed by, "Given what you know about your situation, what's your hunch about which of these, if any, might be an influence?"

Note that an important aspect is generating several possible causal theories, rather than just one. In this way, the dialogue is one of true exploration and more likely to engage thoughtful interaction and long-term learning.

Inviting Thinking

A Sampler of Questions
for Literacy Coaching

BACKGROUND

Thinking cannot be demanded; it must be invited. Thinking out loud, especially if you don't know or are unsure, can feel risky. Literacy specialists must indicate, verbally and nonverbally, that it is OK not to know, at least temporarily. Lipton and Wellman (2003) suggest six elements that increase the invitational quality of the literacy specialist's questions:

The Elements of the Invitation
- Attend Fully
- Use an Approachable Voice
- Use Plural Forms
- Use Exploratory Language
- Apply Positive Presupposition
- Use Nondichotomous Question Forms

Attend Fully

Give your full attention to your colleagues, listening and watching for subtle cues about their emotional readiness for the conversation as well as their perceptions about literacy learning, student development, and your coaching relationship.

Use an Approachable Voice

Intonation signals your intention. A widely modulated inflection pattern that ends on an upward rise, or approachable voice (Grinder, 1995), for paraphrasing and inquiring communicates a spirit of exploration and a desire to engage in open-minded consideration of practice.

Use Plural Forms

Plurals in your questions and paraphrases indicate that there is more than one possibility and increases the options for thinking and responding. This simple syntactical choice invites a colleague to think aloud and generate multiple ideas.

Use Exploratory Language

Partnered with use of plurals, inserting words like *some, might, possible*, and *hunch* into paraphrases and questions widens the range of response and reduced the perceived need for surety. For example, substituting *some* for *the*, as in "What might be *some* causes for this child's behavior?" rather than "*the* causes" increases the willingness to speculate and consider in the moment.

Apply Positive Presuppositions

Presuppositions are messages embedded in our communications but not part of the explicit words we use. A positive presupposition signals our belief in a colleague's professionalism, learning capacity, and willingness to engage. For example, instead of "Can you see anything in this student's writing that meets the standard?" ask "As you examine this student's writing and compare it to the standard, what are some connections you're noticing?"

Use Nondichotomous Question Forms.

Questions that invite thinking are constructed with open-ended, nondichotomous language. A nondichotomous question is one that cannot be answered yes or no. Stems like *do you, have you, can you* shut down thinking and express doubt in readiness or ability. So, by asking what are some effective guided reading strategies that might work here rather than can you think of any guided reading strategies that would work here, your invitation to think automatically communicates your positive presupposition.

98   Questions for Planning

Expert planners differ from less effective or more novice planners in that their plans are goal-oriented and include a clear idea of how goal achievement will be monitored, both formatively and summatively.

The literacy specialist's questions can help form productive habits of mind for instructional planning. Questions that increase awareness about what is expected, how that will be measured, and what will be attended to during an event are powerful teaching tools and provide more enduring learning than any short-term solutions would produce.

Some questions for effective planning include:

- As you think about your (class, lesson, group of students), what are some goals you have in mind?
- What do you expect to see/hear as your outcomes are being achieved?
- What are some things you will pay attention to during this (unit, lesson, event)?
- What are some variables that might influence your actions and outcomes?
- What do you want to be most aware of as you begin this (lesson, unit, event)?
- Based on your previous experiences, what advice would you give to someone who is about to do something similar?
- How will this experience connect with previous and future events?

99   Questions for Reflecting

Reflection is a composite of several cognitive processes, not one large way of operating. Some of the thinking skills involved in reflecting include recollection, summarization, comparison, making inferences, identifying cause-effect, generalizing, and applying.

Some questions you might ask to promote reflection include:

- As you reflect on this experience, where does it fit in the big picture?
- Given your impressions of this event, what might we talk about that would be most useful to you?
- What are some of the things you're noticing about your own reactions to this event?
- As you reflect on your (lesson, presentation, meeting), what are some of the things that come to mind?
- On a scale of 1 to 10, how would you rate this experience?
- On a scale of 1 to 10, how do you think your students would rate this experience?
- As you mentally replay your experiences, what is most vivid?
- What are you most curious about when you recall this experience?
- Describe some of the differences between what you planned and what occurred?
- What are some of your hunches about the reasons for this?
- What are some comparisons you would make between these (students, groups, lessons)?
- What are some inferences you are making about that?
- What are some possible relationships between these?
- What sequence of events might have led to that?
- What are some of the variables that might have affected the outcomes?

- What are some new connections you are making?
- What are some things you are taking away from this experience that will influence your future practice?

100   Questions to Stimulate Discussion

With purposeful syntactic patterns and intentional intonation, your questions can enrich and deepen your collegial conversations. Some effective questions for encouraging learning-focused conversation include:

- What are some of your current questions regarding this aspect of your teaching?
- What are some of your concerns about _____?
- As you think about _____, what captures your attention?
- In what ways does this experience fit within your larger picture for yourself this year?
- What are some experiments you might design to support your own learning?
- What are some of the things that you are learning about (yourself, your students, this curriculum, this unit, this aspect of teaching?)
- What are the most important things a teacher can do to (promote learning, communicate with parents, increase confidence for learners, develop literacy, etc.)?

101   Metaphor and Invention

The mind seeks metaphor and analogy to make meaning. Asking questions that engage our metaphoric brain often result in unexpected or surprising connections. These questions are also psychologically safer than more traditional inquiries because they require invention, and there are clearly no right or wrong responses.

- Imagine you could write a message to yourself and put it in a box that you would open next year. What might it say?
- If this plan were a book, what would the title be? What might the epilogue say?
- If by some edict you could never teach this lesson in the same way again, how might you reinvent it?
- Imagine you are viewing your guided reading lesson through a video camera and it is absolutely successful. What are you seeing that indicates that this is so?
- If you could write a note to yourself at the end of the year and send it to the you that is sitting here right now, what might it say?

References and Further Readings

Allington, R. (2006). *What really matters for struggling readers: Designing research-based programs* (2nd ed.). Boston: Pearson/ Allyn & Bacon.

Anthony, R., Johnson, T., Mickelson, N., & Preece, A. (1991). *Evaluating literacy: A perspective for change.* Portsmouth, NH: Heinemann.

Barton, K., & Smith, L. (2000). Themes or motifs? Aiming for coherence through interdisciplinary outlines. *The Reading Teacher, 54*(1), 54–63.

Beck, I., McKeown, M., & Kucan, L. (2002). *Bringing words to life: Robust vocabulary instruction.* New York: Guilford Press.

Brualdi, A. (2000). Implementing performance assessment in the classroom. *Classroom Leadership Online.* Alexandria, VA: Association for Supervision and Curriculum Development. Retrieved July 14, 2007, from http://www.ascd.org/cms/ objectlib/ascdframeset/index.cfm/publication=http://www .ascd.org/ed_topics/cl200002_brualdi.html

Bellanca, J., & Fogarty, R. (1991). *Blueprints for thinking in the cooperative classroom* (2d ed.). Arlington Heights, IL: IRI/SkyLight Training and Publishing.

Bird, L. (1987). What is whole language? *Teachers Networking: The Whole Language Newsletter, 1,* 1–3.

Brown, R. (1993). *Schools of thought.* San Francisco: Jossey-Bass.

Burke, K. (1994). *How to assess authentic learning.* Arlington Heights, IL: IRI/SkyLight Training and Publishing.

Butler, A., & Turbill, J. (1987). *Toward a reading-writing classroom.* Portsmouth, NH: Heinemann.

Buzzeo, T. (2006). *Read! perform! learn!: 10 reader's theater programs for literacy enhancement.* Ft. Akinson, WI: Upstart Books.

Cambourne, B. (1988). *The whole story: Natural learning and the acquisition of literacy in the classroom.* Richmond Hill, Ontario: Scholastic.

Calkins, L. (2001). *The art of teaching reading.* New York: Addison-Wesley Educational Publishers Inc.

Eisele, B. (1991). *Managing the whole language classroom.* Cypress, CA: Creative Teaching Press.

Fountas, I., & Pinnell, G. S. (2006). *Teaching for comprehending and fluency: Thinking, talking and writing about reading, K–8.* Portsmouth, NH: Heinemann.

Goodman, K. (1989). Whole-language research: Foundations and development. *The Elementary School Journal, 90*(2), 201–223.

Graves, D. (1983). *Writing: Teachers and children at work.* Portsmouth, NH: Heinemann.

Graves, D., & Sunstein, B. (Eds.). (1992). *Portfolio portraits.* Portsmouth, NH: Heinemann.

Grinder, M. (1995). *ENVOY: A personal guide to classroom management.* Battleground, WA: Michael Grinder and Associates.

Harste, J., Short, K., & Burke, C. (1988). *Creating classrooms for authors: The reading-writing connection.* Portsmouth, NH: Heinemann.

Hasbrouck, J., and G. Tindal. 2006. *Oral reading fluency data.* Retrieved on August 15, 2007 from http://www.readnaturally .com/pdf/oralreadingfluency.pdf

Harvey, S., & Goudvis, A. (2007). *Strategies that work: Teaching comprehension for understanding and engagement* (2nd ed.). Portland, ME: Stenhouse.

Hightower, J. (1993, March). Keynote presentation at the Association for Supervision & Curriculum Development National Conference, Chicago.

Hornsby, D., Sukarna, D., & Parry, J. (1986). *Read on: A conference approach to reading.* Portsmouth, NH: Heinemann.

Johnson, D., & Johnson, R. (1988). *Cooperative learning.* The Cooperative Learning Center at University of Minnesota. Minneapolis, MN. Retrieved July 11, 2007, from http://www .co-operation.org/

Keene, E., & Zimmermann, S. (2007). *Mosaic of thought: The power of comprehension strategy instruction* (2nd ed.). Portsmouth, NH: Heinemann.

Langer, J. (2002). *Effective literacy instruction: Building successful reading and writing programs.* Urbana, IL: National Council of Teachers of English.

Lewis, B. (1995). *The kid's guide to service projects*. Minneapolis, MN: Free Spirit Publishing.

Lipton, L., & Wellman, B. (2003). *Mentoring matters: A practical guide to learning-focused relationships*. Sherman, CT: MiraVia, LLC.

Manning, M., & R. Long, R. (1994). *Theme immersions: Inquiry-based curriculum in elementary and middle schools*. Portsmouth, NH: Heinemann.

Marzano, R., Pickering, D., & McTighe, J. (1993). *Assessing student outcomes: Performance assessment using the dimensions of learning model*. Alexandria, VA: Association for Supervision and Curriculum Development.

McCracken, M., & McCracken, R. (1979). Reading, writing and language: A practical guide for primary teachers. Winnipeg: Peguis Publishers.

Miller, D. (2002). *Reading with meaning: Teaching comprehension in the primary grades*. Portland, ME: Stenhouse.

Mueller, J. (2006). Portfolios. *Authentic Assessment Toolbox*. Retrieved July 15, 2007, from http://jonathan.mueller.faculty.noctrl.edu/toolbox/portfolios.html

National Center for Education Statistics. (2000). *National Assessment of Educational Progress*. Washington, DC: Author.

National Endowment for the Arts. (2004). *Reading At risk: A survey of literary reading in America* (Research Division Report No. 46). Washington, DC: Author.

National Reading Panel. (2000). *Put reading first: The research building blocks for teaching children to read*. Rockville, MD: Author. Retrieved June 29, 2007, from http://www.nifl.gov/partnershipforreading/publications/reading_first_print.html

Perkins, D. (1989). Selecting fertile themes for integrated learning. In H. Jacobs (Ed.), *Interdisciplinary curriculum: Design and implementation*. Alexandria, VA: Association for Supervision and Curriculum Development.

Rasinski, T. (2003). *The fluent reader: Oral reading strategies for building word recognition, fluency, and comprehension*. New York: Scholastic.

Rhodes, L., & Shanklin, N. (1993). *Windows into literacy: Assessing learners K–8*. Portsmouth, NH: Heinemann.

Routman, R. (1991). *Invitations: Changing as teachers and learners K–12*. Portsmouth, NH: Heinemann.

Routman, R. (2003). *Reading essentials: The specifics you need to teach reading well*. Portsmouth, NH: Heinemann.

Serafini, F. (2006). *Around the reading workshop in 180 days: A month-by-month guide to effective instruction.* Portsmouth, NH: Heinemann.

Sizer, T. (1992). *Horace's school: Redesigning the American high school.* Boston: Houghton Mifflin.

Trelease, J. (2006). *The read-aloud handbook* (6th ed.). New York: Penguin Press.

Wiggins, G. (2007). *Education topics: Performance tasks.* Alexandria, VA: Association for Supervision and Curriculum Development. Retrieved July 15, 2007, from http://www.ascd.org/portal/site/ascd/menuitem.4427471c9d076deddeb3ffdb62108a0c/template.article?articleMgmtId=759f3f4062520010VgnVCM1000003d01a8c0RCRD

Wood, L. (1997). *Interdisciplinary instruction: A practical guide for elementary and middle school teachers.* Upper Saddle River, NJ: Merrill.

Index